Prisoner 20–801

A French National in the Nazi Labor Camps

Aimé Bonifas

Translated by
Claude R. Foster, Jr., and
Mildred M. Van Sice
from the 4th French
Edition

With a Foreword by
Franklin H. Littell

Southern Illinois
University Press
Carbondale and
Edwardsville

Copyright © 1987 by the Board of Trustees,
Southern Illinois University

Printed in the United States of America

Edited by Teresa White

Designed by Richard Hendel

Production supervised by Natalia Nadraga

Prisoner 20–801 was first published by Editions
Delachaux & Niestlé, Neuchâtel, in 1946 and was
followed by three more French editions in 1966,
1968, 1985; by a Spanish edition in 1949; by
four German editions in 1968, 1972, 1976, 1983;
and by an English edition in 1983.

Library of Congress Cataloging-in-Publication Data

Bonifas, Aimé.

  Prisoner 20–801.

  Translation of: Détenu 20801.

  1. Bonifas, Aimé. 2. World War, 1939–45—
Prisoners and prisons, German. 3. World War,
1939–45—Concentrations camps—Germany.
4. Prisoners of war—Germany—Biography. 4. Prisoners
of war—France—Biography. I. Title. II. Title:
Prisoner 20801.

D805.G3B58613 1987   940.54'72'43   87-2676
ISBN 0-8093-1392-8

Contents

Foreword

For the professing Christian, of all the questions that arise out of study of the Third Reich and the Holocaust the most terrible are these: What were the churches doing? How could such a monstrous crime be committed in the heart of Christendom by baptized Roman Catholics, Protestants, and Eastern Orthodox who were never rebuked, let alone excommunicated? *Where were the Christians?*

Not only were there few Church leaders who showed prophetic courage in the face of nazism, Christian theologians and Church historians who have studied the records are painfully aware that the preaching and teaching of theological anti-Semitism in the Christian churches helped lay the foundations for the Nazi program for "the final solution to the Jewish problem." For the earnest Christian there is little relief in the knowledge that the Nazi anti-Semitism also contained components derived from "Aryan" anthropology and Teutonic tribal myths. A terrorist movement grew from tiny beginnings in the heartland of the Reformation to become a criminal government that dominated Europe from the boot of Italy to the Arctic Circle, from the Dardanelles to the Straits of Dover, from Madrid to the gates of Moscow. And everywhere, during its heyday, it elicited the cheering of mobs of the baptized.

When a few Christian leaders began to find their way out of the maze after the end of the war, they were oppressed by a sense of guilt. At the same time the major Nazi war criminals were pleading "Not Guilty!" at Nuremberg, German churchmen who had actively or passively resisted nazism from 1934 to 1945 were pleading "Guilty!" When newsmen asked the writers of the Stuttgart Declaration of Guilt (October 19, 1945) why they were pleading guilty when they had in fact opposed nazism, the Declaration gave the answer: "We accuse ourselves that we didn't witness more courageously, pray more faithfully, believe more joyously, love more ardently."

Pastor Martin Niemöller was a signer, along with Otto Dibelius, Hanns Lilje, Gustav Heinemann, and others less well known outside Germany. They had long been clear as to the offense of nazism in the establishment of a brutal dictatorship: as early as the Barmen Declaration (May 31, 1934) they had denounced the idolatry of the State. But Dietrich Bonhoeffer, in the end the most consistent and thoroughgoing of the German churchmen who fought nazism, had found little understanding even among his closest allies for his demand that the Church take a forthright stand on behalf of the Jews. When they failed at Barmen he refused to sign the Declaration.

When they met at Stuttgart, in the rubble of Hitler's empire, Hitler's Church opponents were still unable to speak a clear word on Christian responsibility for the war against the Jews. Bonhoeffer was then dead, a martyr. Would he have signed the Stuttgart Declaration?

The awareness of the significance of that failure came later to the Germans and to the ecumenical fellowship. In 1968, within a few weeks of each other, two personalities of the German Church Struggle confessed the failure of the Christian resistance in Germany to understand the importance of the Jewish issue. Eberhard Bethge had just published his biography of Bonhoeffer, and Karl Barth wrote him, "New to me (in your biography) was the fact that Bonhoeffer in 1933 viewed the Jewish question as the first and decisive question, even as the only one, and took it in hand so energetically. I have long felt guilty myself that I did not make this problem central." And Wilhelm Niemöller, brother of the famous pastor and historian of the Church Struggle, opened an article in 1968 with the words: "It has become evident that the Jewish question was actually the *key question* of the Church Struggle. But if we search for the resistance that was raised in the Protestant church in this matter, we come to a miserable result."

The German churchmen had a special problem, of course, for open and unrelenting resistance—especially in time of war—was traditionally called "treason." And the Lutherans had a strong tradition of obedience to the State, placing such obedience next to godliness. Only in the German churches that had a strong Calvinist influence was there any broad opposition to the government; the others, by and large, stayed with the preaching and teaching of docility.

What, however, was the record in other sectors of Christendom—especially in areas where resistance to the German conqueror might express a praiseworthy patriotism as well as Christian belief in the liberty and dignity and integrity of the human person? Unhappily, the report must be critical. The Dutch churches in the end protested; but they were too late to be effective, and there was a vigorous Dutch Nazi party. The Orthodox archbishop of Bulgaria called on his people to protect the Jews, and they did well. The Lutheran archbishop of Denmark did the same. But only in two churches was there any broad and continuing resistance movement: in the Lutheran Church of Norway and the Reformed Church of France.

The place of the French in the history of modern anti-Semitism and fascism is special. The *Dreyfus* case gave a vital impulse to the rise of modern Zionism. If in the 1920s the question had been raised as to where in Europe there might arise a wave of political anti-Semitism, no one would have suggested Germany. The Germans had come to the Jewish villages and ghettoes of the east, at the time of World War I, as deliverers from the persecution and pogroms of the tsars. Rather, on the basis of history, the answer would have been "Poland" or "France." But in point of fact there were two Frances, and had been from the time of the Encyclopedists and the French Revolution.

By the time of World War II there had been two Frances for more than a century and a half. There was the France of traditional loyalties—clerical, anti-Semitic, royalist. And there was the France of the Revolution—anticlerical, secularist, liberal, and cosmopolitan. The one France produced in the nineteenth century some of the most vigorous new orders of Roman Catholic missions and service—and also spawned several reactionary anti-Semitic political associations. The other France was a beacon light to the artistic and literary world, the champion of liberty, equality, and fraternity on the world map—and also a place of weakness toward Marxism as a substitute religion and an alternative system to republican government.

In 1905 the Roman Catholic church lost the special constitutional position it had previously enjoyed. As in most State-Church countries that have adopted a politics of toleration, the populace as a whole was officially religious and in fact emancipated from church loyalties.

With the arrival of the Third Reich, the ideological polarization had destroyed the last remnants of a political consensus. The setting up of the collaborating Vichy regime, headed by the venerable Marshal Pétain, parted the waters both religiously and politically—but along lines that did not always follow the previous fault line. Nevertheless, there is no question but that the Roman Catholic hierarchy—with a few striking exceptions like Eugene Cardinal Tisserant and Archbishop Jules-Gérard Saliège—gave its vigorous or reluctant support to collaboration with Vichy. The spirit that in 1936, in reaction to the Popular Front and the first Jewish French prime minister, announced "better Adolf Hitler than Léon Blum" reached deep into the Church and for a time sustained the Vichy regime, which in a number of matters anticipated German wishes in alacrity of response to anti-Semitic measures.

In the section of France directly occupied by the Germans the situation was different in many respects. But the Vichy area is especially important for the Bonifas story, because the old mountain fastnesses that had once provided bases to the Huguenot struggle in the wars of religion were now to become bases for the militant resistance to the German Occupation. And in the story of the French

Resistance, both passive and armed, the French Protestants played an especially important role.

Pastor Bonifas belongs in a great tradition, a tradition that produced some of the first significant Christian books on the Christian duty of resistance to an illegitimate government and to immoral actions by a legitimate government. The Church resistance within the Germany of the Third Reich came primarily from those centers that had been influenced by Calvinism. In France the Reformed Church stood solidly in the Calvinist line of interpretation of Christian truth and its application to government and individual civic duty.

Like the Trocmé family of Le Chambon, Aimé Bonifas grew up in the Reformed tradition. He studied theology and worked in student and YMCA circles during years when men like Pierre Maury, Marc Boegner, Hendrik Kraemer, Willem Visser't Hooft, and Reinhold Niebuhr were putting their mark on the ecumenical movement. They represented a recovery of biblical theology in the tradition of the Reformation of the sixteenth century. They laid the foundations for a new Christian theological orientation toward the Jewish people. They were unflinchingly opposed to the idolatry of the state—with its murderous consequences—represented by nazism. They were equipped with Confessions of Faith that made Christian resistance not only a right but sometimes an inescapable duty. They had, in the years before World War II, built a worldwide network of prayer, friendship, and concern that would sustain those members of the national movements that came under the hammer as resisters. As the battle of the resisters went on, in the churches and on the political scene, the awareness grew of the close connection between tyranny and anti-Semitism on the one hand and liberty and Christian-Jewish understanding and empathy on the other.

Aimé Bonifas' story fills a valuable place in the modern history of Christian witness under adversity, in a situation where patriotism and faith, devotion and courage were finely blended.

Franklin H. Littel

Preface

Since the period recalled in this book, there have been so many other wars, so many camps, so much enslavement, torture, massacre, unfathomable suffering! Is it necessary to evoke again these events?

Now while the last survivors are still among us, many people do not yet know or suspect the extent of the crime. Furthermore, for several years attempts to falsify history and to present nazism as a commonplace have been manifested persistently in statements, magazine articles, books, seminars.

This pseudoscientific approach of the "revisionists," which in reality has not a historic but an ideological objective, is not taken seriously by serious historians, who compose the great majority. But the revisionist endeavor becomes tragically serious in its capacity for instilling doubt in the minds of the uninformed.

Those of us who suffered from the excesses of nazism cannot restrain ourselves from reporting what we have seen and endured. Furthermore, we owe our public outcry to those who can no longer bear witness.

For the first time in history, in the middle of the twentieth century we have witnessed a horror carefully planned and executed, a programmed death industry. At a time of economic and moral crisis, Hitler and his accomplices, taking advantage of the frustrations of the German people and supported by influential interests wanting to exploit Hitler's paranoia, intended—among other things—to efface a race of people from the earth. If the effort had been allowed to suceed, other peoples were to have been either exterminated or mercilessly enslaved.

Nazism is a nihilistic ideology. The monstrous crimes that it engendered in the name of the superman myth and of racial purity were not produced accidentally: they were inherent in the logic of the system. Its totalitarian, demiurgic, Promethean claim issued from the most profound paganism.

Hitler's concentration camps, the *chef-d'œuvre* of the system, represent something beyond a dark chapter in history, beyond a cyclone of terror followed only by numbering the dead and taking account of the spoils. Never to be forgotten is this satanic endeavor that not only consumed the life of millions of human beings but even brought into question the destiny of the species. As André Malraux wrote: "The problem that arises for us, today, is to know whether or not, on this old European soil, man is dead. . . . Torture signified for us much more than pain." And another question gusted from the whirling storm: Where is God?

Ah! The silence of God at the brink of death! That is perhaps indeed the ultimate test. If the angel stopped the arm of Abraham at the moment when he was going to sacrifice his son as a burnt offering, at Auschwitz millions of Isaacs were sacrificed and the word of the Lord did not sound forth. And elsewhere, for forty years, men like André Neher or Elie Wiesel have not ceased to question the silence of God.

The questioning of Job or of Jeremiah or of others who testify to the Word by which all things were made has never ceased to resound through the history of the human race. Who has never felt in sympathy with and touched by their rebellion against an incomprehensible suffering or an absurd fate? Too many children, young men, and young women have fallen prey to intolerable suffering at the hands of an evil that has snatched them away; too much happiness has been irretrievably destroyed; too many homes have been broken.

But the silence is not the absence of God; it is at least His provisional way of being there. As St. John of the Cross explained, "The Father has spoken only one word and He always speaks it in an unending silence: this word is His Son." How eloquent is the silence of the Son before Pilate, the silence of the Father at the Golgotha of His Son!

Not until many centuries later was Job's question answered through another victim: that righteous One who knew the same situation, the same silence, the same abandonment. Through His and by His unjust death, that which had been meaningless and cruel suddenly acquired meaning, for—"strange love which even rebellion cannot ignore," in the words of Camus—it is here that Jesus inscribed in the history of mankind the answer: a love without reciprocity, which freely bestows its radiant favor with such assurance of ultimate victory that death itself will be forever destroyed by this love.

Through all our suffering a Love crucified and yet victorious mysteriously travels with us. From the defeat of Auschwitz sprang forth hope through the rebirth of the people of the promise.

Nevertheless, the memory of the past must set us on guard and sustain our vigilance. The temptation of totalitarianism can appear in various guises. The diseases of racism, anti-Semitism, xenophobia, can be reactivated at any moment. In our pluralistic democracies, where tolerance and solidarity remain tenuous, where deteriorating social conditions push the middle class to the point of despair, there is a climate favorable to a population predisposed, under pretext of maintaining order, to venture such experiments as a "providential leader" might advocate.

Even now the disease of nazism exists in its dormant stage. That is why it is still necessary to instruct and to train the young not for a society governed by the tyranny of regimes founded on contempt for man but for a society based on respect for the dignity of man and for his basic freedoms.

The following account is not a journal kept in the camp: we had neither paper nor pencil nor time to withdraw and take notes. Aside from a few corrections of details, these pages appear as they were spontaneously written, upon my return, not for publication but simply for my family. I have preserved the sobriety of these recollections, and I have not wanted to enhance them with sensational descriptions.

This is a testimony in first-person singular, though hundreds of thousands of prisoners from all the European nations, beginning with those from Germany, suffered the same fate. For each one, obviously, the common fate produced a personal experience. Nevertheless, these memoirs would not have been published if I were not sure that each of my comrades, or for that matter any prisoner from any Nazi concentration camp, would recognize herein his own lot. Indeed, this simple testimony has attracted, in various countries, an audience that I could not have imagined.

Since that time, even if the memory of the horror lives within me, I have had the good fortune of marrying, establishing a family, exercising a pastoral ministry that has filled my life. International responsibilities have taken me across Europe and have multiplied my contacts and friendships, especially with the German people. Although I continue to marvel at such a postwar life as I have been granted by grace, I remain inconsolable, along with the families of my comrades, at the disappearance of so many brothers and friends into the terrifying night of martyrdom.

The number of French deportees in the concentration camps of the Third Reich was about 230,000, of whom 80,000 were Jews. Most of the others were members of the Resistance or political dissenters, but there were also victims of the sweeps and some criminals who had been sentenced to hard labor. Only 30,000 returned from these camps, often in a very enfeebled state.

Since such a large number of the French deportees were Jews, it may be surprising that I do not speak of the treatment of Jews in particular in these camps. The Jews who were with us at Compiègne—and who were, for us, simply French like the rest of us— were sent to the camp of Drancy, then transferred to Auschwitz. When I arrived at Buchenwald in September 1943, the Jews who previously had been there had already been exterminated, and I noticed only two or three stars of David. In the commandos to which I was then assigned, there were no Jews or at least no individuals recognized as Jews.

In addition to those who were sent to the concentration camps, many young Frenchmen were sent to Germany as workers. Le Service du Travail Obligatoire en Allemagne (S.T.O. [the Service of Compulsory Labor]), created in 1942 by order of the Occupation authorities, registered for conscripted labor in the German war factories all young men born in 1920, 1921, or 1922. Only a few of these young people had the means or the will to evade the draft. In early 1943, these few reached the forests, the high plateaus, the mountains, and they significantly reinforced the Maquis units then forming.

However, it was in the summer of 1940 that we had begun to organize the first Resistance networks. Yet, despite the early inception of the Resistance movement, I should not wish to imply that all the French actively resisted the Occupation force, servant of a perverse ideology. In the beginning there was only a handful who resisted, and even if their number was greatly increased after the Allied landing in North Africa and the total Axis occupation of France in November 1942, those engaged in clandestine and dangerous acts always constituted a minority. On the other hand, there were in France some "collaborators," ranging from devoted admirers of the old Marshal Pétain's prestige to adherents of frankly Fascist movements. The French police often (fortunately not always) were accomplices in the Gestapo's repressive acts, and to our great shame there was even a French regiment of Waffen-SS. But the masses, preoccupied with the urgent needs of daily life, were composed of those with a wait-and-see attitude; they were victims of circumstance, and they hailed liberation with sincere relief.

Among the few who were active in the Resistance were a number of women, whose role can never be overestimated. They participated in the humblest tasks as well as in the most audacious, and they were, for example, efficient couriers. Anna Seghers, the German novelist, said in speaking of the women of Ravensbrück, the largest women's camp in the Nazi regime: "They are mothers and sisters to all of us. You would not be able to study freely or to play, perhaps you would not even have been born, if these women had not protected you with their frail bodies, as if with a bronze buckler, for the duration of the Fascist reign of terror."

Although the men and women who dared resist were few in number, their contribution was significant. As General Eisenhower declared, the role of the French Resistance in slowing down the arrival of German reinforcements when the Allies landed on Normandy in June 1944 was considerable.

I hope that I have not succumbed to the absurdity of chauvinism, for, though I love my country, the land of my forefathers, I know well that national arrogance is blindness. But please try to imagine to what extent, during those years, the French nation and we who were identified as French were attacked, humiliated, considered worthy only of contempt. I rejoiced every time the insult was belied by the facts.

What I say about stressful relationships between prisoners of various nationalities may trouble the reader who is uninformed about the unscrupulous mixing of incompatible camp populations. As the occasion has presented itself, I have expressed my gratitude for Belgian, Czechoslovakian, German, or Russian comrades, for example, and for others also. But it must be acknowledged that through misunderstanding and even hostility we were at odds with certain Russians and Poles. Most French deportees in the various camps have made the same allegation.

As painful as that was for us, we can find explanations, and responsibility certainly is not unilateral. The Poles who "welcomed" us (for they were usually members of the self-government staff) in 1943 had already finished three years of hard labor and had survived, under duress, most often by serving the system. Most of the

Russians whom I knew, aside from a few magnificent exceptions, were young Ukrainians who had lived through the terrible misfortunes of the war in their country by stealing and plundering. Among them there were few if any truly committed to the Resistance. But it is not by the conduct of a few individuals in exceptional circumstances that a people can be judged, and it is not my intention to make such a judgment.

Some Marxist historians have a tendency to convey the impression that the prisoners from the various nations were all participants in the Resistance movement and were united in total solidarity by their opposition to the Fascist enemy. The reality was more complex. The diabolical genius of the Nazi concentration camp organizers must be recognized in the practice of grouping with criminals the Resistance members, political dissenters, and those imprisoned because of race; and of bringing together those speaking different languages and of various nationalities. The explicit purpose was to divide us, to set us against each other, and to metamorphose us into stags staging a standoff.

If, in certain large camps such as Buchenwald, the political and Resistance prisoners could at times seize control by subduing the criminals, thereby putting an end to certain kinds of extortion, this was not the case in the commandos that I knew, where we were at the mercy not only of the SS but also of the servile and sadistic criminals in the position of kapos, or chiefs.

Finally, to those intimidated by the pessimism and discouragement that the reading of such an account as the following might engender, I should like to say that this is also a lesson in confidence and hope that surmounts the ordeal of the camps. If man is capable of baseness and unqualified cruelty, he is also capable, even in disorienting conditions of terror and abandon, of acts of solidarity and of self-sacrifice. If their executioners destroyed the flesh of my comrades, most of the victims did not surrender their conscience.

The Resistance was at first a spiritual insurrection. Each received the inspiration after his own fashion, depending on his concept of man and of society and on his ideology or his faith. In my case, I have often invoked my seventeenth-century Huguenot ancestors, imprisoned for having reasserted their freedom of conscience, who engraved in the stone of their prison, "résistez"! Is not theirs the necessary stance if men are to stand tall, free, and independent?

Prisoner 20–801

Flight

I know the fountain which wells up and flows even at night.

—St. John of the Cross, mystical poems.

Bong, bong, bong, bon-n-ng. . . . This is London. Frenchmen speaking to Frenchmen.

So it all begins. Across borders, through fog, penetrating the strange, dull silence that oppresses city and countryside, a somber voice speaks to us of hope.

In that autumn of 1940 our country was paralyzed by an unprecedented military defeat that threatened our national identity and even our honor. I was twenty years old. My age group, drafted two weeks before France capitulated, received a military discharge from the induction center. We were defeated without having fought. Two million of us were behind barbed wire in Germany. Every day the burden of enemy occupation was becoming more oppressive, multiplying vexations and increasing our bitterness. Most enraging was the propaganda of neoconformism, which all day, every day, slandered the underlying principles of our culture and way of life.

I was finishing my law studies at Montpellier, a haven for Alsatian students—Montpellier, where de Lattre, the local commander at the hotel command post, boldly ordered the changing of the guard to the triumphant beat of the Lorraine march.

Very soon a group of us, gathered around a rasping old radio, formed a conspiracy. The example of the Free French, under the command of General de Gaulle, inspired us to dream of promoting the cause of liberty. We had lost a battle, not the war! How difficult it was at that time to preserve such a faith! But our youth enabled us to implement that faith. At first, we naïvely drew Lorraine crosses on walls, scribbled graffiti that attacked the Germans or ridiculed the Italians, and slipped messages into mailboxes. Opposing the

3

general resignation, we determined to resurrect the will to resist. My professor, Pierre Henri Teitgen, was well qualified to help us. Under his direction we formed the first "Combat" group, dedicated first of all to propaganda. Completely ignorant of the risk involved, I took charge of distribution of the underground newspaper in Nîmes.

The following year, after I had earned my degree, in an effort to give meaning to my life I joined the Young Men's Christian Association, a Protestant youth movement which sponsored many meetings, camps, and other activities. In the prevailing demoralizing atmosphere of complicity, of opportunism, and of the pervasive black market, it was edifying to meet young people still inspired by an ideal. During this time I completed a six-month training course at the National Staff College in Uriage. The course was under the direction of Dunoyer de Segonzac, the old officer whom we would have followed through thick and thin. While I was still in Uriage, Laval announced on the radio: "I am in favor of a German victory." This pronouncement sounded the death knell of the apparent respect that our school had held for the old Marshal Pétain. Not long thereafter the corps left school to form resistance groups.

Events then followed with an inexorable logic. The South Zone was occupied, foreign refugees on our territory were turned over to the enemy, Jews were deported, roundups were initiated, and hostages were shot. Resistance groups, still limited to a few admirably courageous men, were being organized. Guerilla bands were formed in the regions of Corrèze and Vercors. When the opportunity arose, we disseminated counterpropaganda, gathered intelligence, and concealed Jews. The occupation forces, with the help of the Vichy collaborators, instituted the Service of Compulsory Labor in Germany (Le Service de Travail Obligatoire en Allemagne [S.T.O.]). Since I had persuaded several eligible young men that we should evade conscription by the S.T.O., my situation as an itinerant became uncomfortable because of the many police sweeps and identity checks. The clouds gathered over our unhappy fatherland, and we sensed that the hour of reckoning drew near when we must drive the hated field gray from our soil. I determined to become more active by joining the North African Army that had been organized after the Anglo-American landing. I could have gone to Switzerland to study theology, toward which I felt impelled, but my conscience would have condemned as defection such a course of action. Like many others, I planned to reach Algeria through Spain. Reliable friends, students at the theological faculty in Montpellier, had established an escape route over the Pyrenees. At two-week intervals this route had been used, so far without incident.

At the end of May 1943, having made my decision, I went to Lyon to arrange my affairs. On Sunday I went to the Lanterne Street Chapel, to that congregation that had inspired me. I arrived just as my friend, the Pastor Roland de Pury, still in his ecclesiastical robe, was led away between two civilians, who forced him into an automobile. Not only the clarity and courage of his sermons but also his clandestine activity had earned him the honor of being arrested by the Gestapo just before the worship service was to begin. Before the empty chancel stood a bewildered congregation. Children were there with their parents and friends; it was confirmation Sunday.

One Friday, a few days after I had concluded all arrangements at Lyon, Nîmes, and Montpellier, I put on sturdy walking shoes and packed some provisions in a knapsack. Andrew Lew accompanied me by train from Montpellier to Foix (Ariège), where he entrusted me to the guide who was to smuggle me into Spain. This guide, an automobile mechanic from Varilhes, was waiting in his car at the railroad station exit. I was not alone; seven other young men were keeping the same rendezvous. Among them was Albert Cappus, who became my very dear friend.

Our guide drove us by back roads to the forbidden zone, parked his car, and joined us for the long march across the border. The light rain, which had been falling since morning, stopped. In a single, silent file we gradually gained the high country. Night had already fallen when we came to a halt by a lake where another group awaited us; there were now eighteen of us. Most of my hiking companions were fleeing forced labor in Germany. Some had no ambition other than to escape to some secure haven and there to await the course of events. Some, in dress shoes and without provisions, seemed to regard this expedition in a cavalier manner. Their nonchalance contributed to their lack of perseverance.

We walked in the high valleys all through the night—a splendid night of twinkling stars, a night filled with the strange tenderness of springtime. Our guide informed us that we had already passed the first line of German border posts. Toward morning, however, our march was delayed. Twelve of our companions who could not maintain the pace fell behind. The guide lost a great deal of time looking for them. At daybreak we had still not crossed the border. Our guide, who was becoming uneasy, tried to conceal us behind cliffs, but cover in this region under German surveillance was difficult. Soon it was broad daylight and to come out of hiding before nightfall was out of the question.

Suddenly, behind us, shots rang out, followed by guttural commands. The German border guards had sighted us through their binoculars and surprised us from behind while we were trying to conceal outselves from the valley posts that lay before us. Since we were within firing range of the Germans, we could not flee. If we had known what was awaiting us, we, no doubt, would have tried. Fortunately we were widely scattered among the rocks, and only nine of us were seen and captured.

Thus our escape attempt failed because of the physical and moral deficiency of some of the members of our group and because of the irresolution which resulted. It is also possible that our group was reported while we were traveling through certain hamlets. However, if we had forced the march, we would have crossed the border. Ironically my only concern had been to avoid Franco's prisons. I spoke Spanish, I had three or four addresses in Catalonia, and I had some pesetas.

It was Pentecost, June 13, 1943, 8:30 A.M., at an altitude of 2,800 meters. The border was only two kilometers away. A new chapter opened.

Driven down the slopes by guards who never removed a finger from the trigger, I pondered my ill-fated plans. At first I remained calm. The conviction that I had voluntarily chosen a course of action compatible with duty fostered a serenity lacking in those who had dreamed only of escaping difficulties. However, great anguish arose in me when I thought of the pain that the news of my arrest would bring to my family and friends.

After a three-hour march, with our packs cutting into our shoulders and our shoes rubbing our feet, we arrived in the charming little city of Aulus-les-Bains. At the Grand Hotel we were greeted by a loud and overbearing Gestapo official, the very type of German often caricatured by the Alsatian illustrator Hansi. Frisking and the first interrogation, rites often to be repeated during the time of our captivity! Mistakenly, Eychenne was thought to be our guide. The Gestapo, by crushing his testicles, tried to force him to confess, but Eychenne remained silent!

We were then placed under heavy guard on the hotel lawn, and, exhausted, we stretched out on the grass. We had been on our feet for twenty-four hours. Now we wanted to think of nothing, to spend Sunday afternoon on this tender grass, and to gaze at the snowy peaks glorified by a brilliant sun. No longer to think of anything! If only there had not been those ever-present, greenish-gray uniforms!

About 5:00 P.M. the weather became unpleasant and a thunder storm of unusual intensity raged on the mountain. How were our scattered companions up there protecting themselves? Much later I learned that most of them, including the Dutch chargé d'affaires in London, who had joined our group, had crossed the border to freedom. To think that, if there had been no delay, we too would have escaped detection by the border guards! But regret is futile. It does not help to complain. We must face our destiny.

The lady who ran the hotel received permission from our "gentlemen captors" to bring us coffee, which was certainly welcomed. She served us; she was very upset and did not know how to express her sympathy. I succeeded in scribbling on a piece of paper the address of my family and in slipping it to her discreetly so that she could notify my relatives. Searching for words of comfort, she assured us that the war would soon be over. Brave French woman, our last comforting contact with the free world, whom we remembered with gratitude!

In the late afternoon we were loaded onto an army truck that had been sent for us. We traveled at a high speed along a narrow road. Saint-Girons: after the customary frisking the door of the prison closed on our little group.

There we were, now forced to begin a new life together. What would it bring us? Where would it end? Shoulder to shoulder, we united in the face of difficulty. This spirit of solidarity prompted us to share our remaining provisions.

Behind Prison Walls

Where the absurdity of suffering exists, there exists also the possibility of scandal, which is inseparable from the Christian condition.

—Søren Kierkegaard,
Training in Christianity

To have dreamed of adventure—to rush to scale peaks, to be in love with the wide open spaces and with light as we were at our age—and to find ourselves in a sort of vault with dense walls constituted a quite unexpected turn of events.

Our prison, like all prisons, I suppose, was dirty and dark, and the walls were covered with graffiti. From the ceiling a dormer window complete with solid bars allowed a dull light to filter through. During the following days, using the scaffolding made from our beds, we climbed to the bars, and for hours we remained there to contemplate a deserted courtyard—surrounded by a high wall, stifling the sounds of the city—and the top of a tree against the corner of blue sky. This scene induced reminiscence, and the music of Verlaine overwhelmed me with a haunting nostalgia:

> Against the sky so blue and calm
> Above the loft,
> A tree waves her palm
> In breezes soft.
> "What have you done, you there,
> Shedding endless tears?
> What have you done, you there,
> With your young and tender years?"

The only defense against the melancholy of this forced inactivity was contemplation. "Your strength will be made perfect through tranquillity and trust." Yet we were glad that we were not in separate cells.

Our first night passed well. We were too sleepy to worry about broken bedsprings or dusty straw mattresses. We awakened in the morning on June 14, 1943, and, as our second day of captivity began, we waited—for whom or for what? We knew nothing. We were waiting for something to happen. Thus, for two years, all of our days would be filled with waiting. The waiting prevented our resignation to a present that was temporary.

Jean Rieg, with a pencil, drew a calendar on the wall and marked a cross through the first day, already spent.

Finally, toward the middle of the morning, a guard's footsteps echoed through the corridor. Another typical prison sound that we would soon know well followed—the grating of the key in the heavy lock and the rattling of all the other keys on the ring.

Revolver in hand, a young SS guard with a bestial face confronted us. He led away the prisoner who had arrived first and, still jingling his keys, closed the massive door. A half-hour later, it was someone else's turn. Approximately every half-hour—what a long time is a half-hour!—the same routine began again until the last occupant of our cell had been led away. My turn came after Albert's.

Fearfully, I walked ahead of the guard with the revolver. He directed me through the corridors, and, stopping in front of one cell, he had me look through the peephole at Albert, whose nose was bleeding. My guard gave me to understand that he had struck my comrade in the face because Albert would not talk, and the guard threatened me with similar treatment if I should demonstrate a reluctance to answer his questions. Thus I was introduced to my first SS guard.

I was brought before a Gestapo agent who spoke French. He explained sententiously that he was going to interrogate me, that my answers would be carefully verified, and that if I should make false statements, the worst possible punishments awaited me. Anxiously I wondered what he wanted to know from me, and I determined not to give the name of my associates. Fortunately, I was very calm. I was obliged to fill out a long questionnaire about my civilian status, my studies, my profession, my home—a questionnaire that asked for such insignificant details as "age entered in nursery school." But there was almost nothing about the motive or the purpose of my trip to Spain. For fear that my relatives would be harrassed, I made the most absurd declarations. I had to sign the form in triplicate. Verification of my statements was never made. What bureaucracy! No one informed us of our sentence, and we would not have understood its implications. Eychenne, who had already been a prisoner of war and had escaped, and who spoke a few words of German, tried to learn what our fate would be. A guard told him that we would be sent to the Reich to work in the most modern factories, that we would be well paid, and that we would have excellent food. But these idealized descriptions, circulated as propaganda by the Nazis and the Vichy collaboration, left us more than skeptical.

We remained at Saint-Girons for three days—three relatively tranquil days. The door opened in the morning, and we were allowed five minutes of recreation in the yard. During this recreation break we were allowed to wash ourselves at the spigot. Once again we were frisked and deprived of almost all of our personal possessions: watch, pen, money. (As a precaution, I had brought with me a fairly large sum of money.) Naturally, we were never to see these items again. The SS paid well. It was a sort of institutionalized banditry.

During these first three days absolutely nothing was brought to us to eat, and our provisions were exhausted. After several complaints to our guards, they ordered for us from a local restaurant an excellent meal of meat, vegetables, and wine, which we greatly appreciated. But our confiscated money lavishly repaid them!

On the fourth day, in the morning, we were led out, our bags in hand, and penned into a truck. We traveled toward Toulouse. We had spent only three days in prison, but we yearned to be free. Through the gaps between the planks of the truck, we could see Saint-Girons and the neighboring countryside. The view reassured us.

The truck slowed down in the traffic of Toulouse and stopped. We climbed out in front of a large building on which was written "Military Prison." At the entrance, French guards took charge of us. Again we were searched, and the few worthless treasures that had been left to us were taken away: paper, envelopes, pencils, a knife, razor blades, tobacco, shoelaces. Each search deprived us further.

We were led into a small first-floor cell, directly facing the yard. Four wooden bunks constituted all of the furniture. The ninth prisoner of our group was lodged in the neighboring cell; however, we could communicate through a hole in the brick wall. Later, a bed was added to our little cell, and a very congenial Polish officer, arrested for espionage (he had transmitted intelligence to London), became our cell mate. Then, after several days, Albert was sent to a cell on the second floor, and a second Polish prisoner took his place. In spite of these two separations, our little group sensed a growing solidarity. Although there were marked differences in our background and education, we felt united by a common destiny.

Prison caused not only time but also space to become ever-present reality. Alas, we could at a glance survey our estate. Our cell was almost entirely filled with beds, and the free floor space hardly permitted us to take more than three or four steps. And there were nine of us! In the corner stood the indispensable bucket, because we were allowed to leave the cell only once a day. The first day, the Polish officer felt obliged to apologize for using this receptacle in our presence. We were to witness many such scenes henceforth.

The window of our cell opened onto the yard, and our main distraction was to observe what was happening out there. Finally, we knew by sight all the prisoners who had been granted the right of a daily walk. They appeared in successive groups, about three hundred in all. We noticed the newcomers, and we worried about those who were missing. There were many differences, but the charges against most of the prisoners were of two classifications: black market and resistance. A few had been arrested by chance in the police roundups; others had not had their identification papers in order. There were several foreigners and even a German deserter—a poor, red-haired boy, who awaited his execution.

Some of the prisoners appeared to be of reputable social standing; several wore decorations. Some women were imprisoned on the third floor. They were being held because of their participation in the resistance, as aliens, because of their black market activities, or on morals charges. They were much more excitable than were the men. The women spoke loudly and laughed nervously. They could adapt even less well to this dim nether world.

We discovered that several prisoners, unable to stand because they had been so abused by the Gestapo during the interrogations designed to force confessions, remained stretched out on their mattresses. We heard about the torture chamber methods: blows, ice baths, hanging by the feet or by the wrists tied behind the back, etc. We began to comprehend the immensity of the drama acted out daily in the cellars of the Gestapo quarters. Ah! How we wished that we could shout out all that we heard here, while Vichy continued to play the pitiful tragicomedy of collaboration!

Time began to drag unbearably. We became preoccupied with our hunger. Our diet consisted of a quart of coffee and about 250 grams of bread in the morning, a very clear soup and a vegetable at noon, and an inadequate serving of a boiled vegetable in the evening. Although we did not work, the food was insufficient. We impatiently waited for mealtime. My comrades put me in charge of food distribution. Meticulously I apportioned the rations. I had to be as fair as possible, since each gram counted.

The inactivity, the insufficient diet, the isolation, began to undermine our resistance. Through entire afternoons, I remained stretched out on my bed, a prey to violent migraine headaches.

The crucial question that nobody any longer dared to ask, since we all knew that the same question haunted everyone, was, How much longer?

Waiting for news was second only to waiting for food. When we were arrested, the Allies had just landed at Pantelleria, a small island off Sicily, and we felt sure that, as a harbinger of the liberation of the Continent, the anticipated occupation of Italy would take place within the next few days. Many rumors circulated among the prisoners. Sung to popular tunes, the gossip was passed from window to window. Most of the time the reports were without foundation. Nobody knew what gave rise to them, but they sounded like the truth right up to the moment when they burst like soap bubbles. It was the prison environment that prompted such fabrications, spawned them, demanded them, nourished them. A newspaper—nobody knew how it got into the prison—gave us the German version of the news. We discovered to our great disappointment that the situation was stationary. Nevertheless, we could not help believing that an important and decisive move was being prepared by the Allies. But we wanted to know. And we began to dream about the moment when the advance of our armies would open prison doors and would chase the invader from this soil that he had made to bleed but could never enslave.

I felt sorry for Eychenne, who craved tobacco. I do not know how he succeeded in procuring matches. He smoked whenever he could find anything to smoke. He scraped bits of tobacco from the bottom of his pocket or from the bowl of his pipe and rolled the scrapings in newspaper. He also rolled bits of straw. He paced like a wild animal in a cage. What would he not have given for a *Gauloise?*

In spite of the successive searches, Carestia had succeeded in keeping a deck of cards. I was introduced to the mysteries of *couanche* and of *belote,* and we played endless tournaments by teams.

But, above all, I was able to keep the pocket Bible given to me when I joined the church. On the flyleaf, my aunt had written: "Wait upon the Lord and He will strengthen thine heart" and "I am with you always and will watch over you wherever you go." Were not these the two promises I needed in order to live? These promises were a comfort to my disquieted heart, and they were especially applicable to my particular circumstances. God's grace would enable me to put these promises to the test, even in the darkest hours.

Seated on a corner of the bed, I passed away the time by reading the Bible again, especially the epistles of Saint Paul. By reading a whole book at a time, the reader grasps the spirit of the pages. And then there are the Psalms, the enrapturing Psalms. There are many ordinary ways of listening to the Psalms—in the rhythm of the old liturgies, for example. But imagine what reading the Psalms can mean to a prisoner, to a man who is behind locked doors, who knows the distress that inspired most of David's psalms. The cry "Out of the Depths" is not just words. The prisoner spontaneously cries, "Have mercy on us! Deliver us!"

Piled on top of one another as we were, it was not possible to lose oneself in reading without being noticed. My comrades questioned me about the Bible and about what Protestants believe. Aside from one of them, who was a devout Catholic, they knew almost nothing about traditional Christianity. Indeed, while it is difficult in the normal circumstances of life tactfully to introduce a discussion of religion, here the subject was not only acceptable but attractive. As the Oxford Group says: "Man's failure is God's opportunity." I had the pleasure, at least during the first few days, of being with Albert. Many common interests brought us together: our age, the same studies, and our association with the Federation of Christian Students, which had nourished our faith. A very strong friendship developed between us. We read the Bible together, and our fellow prisoners joined us. By explaining important points, I tried to review for them what I had learned. Thus we spent much of our time in improvised Bible study. The Jewish question in particular and the mystery of this people of Israel especially attracted our attention. Our comrades asked if nazism and all the gyrations of history would escape the final judgment of the Lord of History.

As much for pastime, no doubt, as for the satisfaction of spiritual need (Who can know?), each one read long passages from the Bible. I attempted, without intellectual argumentation, simply to tell my fellow prisoners what the person of Jesus Christ meant to me. I believe that some of them discovered that faith is not an empty dream but a living reality for those who receive it. Thus the first Sunday—I do not remember whether on my initiative or at their suggestion—I conducted a short worship service, including some elements of the liturgy that I explained to them, the reading of some passages from the Bible, and a meditation. Our common prayer petitioned God for deliverance, but above all else for submission to His will. Thus in spite of walls and barred doors, this obscure cell in Toulouse became a sanctuary. God is there, wherever two or three are gathered together in His name. This worship service, which before their imprisonment might have brought forth a sneer from the participants, provided great comfort and reinforced our friendship.

Suddenly, in the monotony of our life, we became preoccupied with the question of departure. To tell the truth, no one knew anything about it. Nevertheless, the rumor persisted that, after a layover of two or three days at Compiègne, we would be sent to Germany. In fact, on July 1, very early, our doors were opened and we were mustered in the yard. After we received travel rations, German police took charge of us. A large supply of handcuffs lay at hand. The roll was called in alphabetical order, and we were linked together two by two. For thirty hours, all the way to Compiègne, we remained chained together, unable to detach ourselves even to attend to our natural needs, which could not be satisfied in privacy.

Trucks transported us to the freight entrance of the railroad station. (There are some sights from which the public must be shielded!) Fortunately the Société Nationale des Chemins de Fer Français (S.N.C.F.) had reserved comfortable passenger cars for us, but in spite of the accommodations, the trip was to be very unpleasant. Naturally, each compartment was guarded. We could not take our eyes off the throng that crowded the platforms on this first day of the vacation season! Indeed, there were still those who could go on vacation.

Under a blazing sun, which flooded the countryside, the train crossed meadows, rivers, fields of grain, and villages throughout France. Montauban, Cahors (where Albert caught sight of his parents' house with the shutters half closed), Limoges, stations where women in summer dresses were waiting, groups of children: vacation, life!

At six o'clock in the evening we pulled into bustling Paris-Austerlitz. A dense, swarming throng crowded the suburban trains. Red Cross volunteers went through our car during the stop and did their best to hand out provisions: bread and sardines and, most important of all, water. (We were very thirsty.) Our train was pushed onto a siding. Then all night long we were jolted about on the great Parisian track network, and we hardly closed our eyes. I do not know whether or not there were guards posted along the rails; there probably were none. I believe that I could have slipped away from our guard if I had not been handcuffed to another prisoner.

The sun rose again on the Parisian suburb, on the peaceful setting of flower gardens and wooded areas.

Compiègne, Detention Camp

*We do not ask that the grain under the grindstone
Be returned to the sheaf.*

—Péguy,
    petition

Toward noon, our train arrived in the station of Compiègne, where an impressive police reception awaited us, if one may put it that way! In closed ranks, still chained together, we marched through the whole city. As people made way at our approach, the emotion expressed in their faces said much about their sentiments. For three years, Compiègne had been under military occupation, and the citizens understood the meaning of Nazi rule.

The camp, surrounded by observation posts and barbed wire, had been constructed on the outskirts of the city on a site known as Royal-Lieu (Royal Place)—what an irony! Once we passed through the entrance, we were finally detached from one another and sequestered in a barrack until someone came to take charge of us. Soon afterward, always quite correct (the Germans conducted themselves with decorum as long as we were in France), some soldiers mustered us in order to complete the formality of registration. Another search deprived me of the stationery that I had guarded jealously. Once again we were required to fill out a questionnaire so that a file could be established for us, and each of us was given a prison badge. Henceforth, I was number 16160 of the front stalag, number 122. Having received a mess tin and a spoon, we were led to the interior of the camp.

How astonished and jubilant we were to observe, on the vast terrain extending within the perimeter of the camp, prisoners strolling, playing sports, and sunbathing! Finally, a little space! Finally, one could go out, walk, run, and see other faces. The walls of our prison gave place to what seemed to us a semiliberty, since we were no longer confined to our cells.

A prisoner was assigned to oversee our installation. We were directed to building A-3, room 9. We were especially pleased that our group of nine was not fragmented; because of our friendship and our instinct for self-defense, we wanted to remain together.

The prisoners themselves, under the supervision of the Germans, assumed responsibility for the internal organization of the camp. At the head was the "dean" of the camp, a Communist teacher, who had been there for several months and who spoke German. Each building was managed by a building chief, supported by a secretary, policemen, and ration distributors. Discipline was lax, but order reigned by tacit accord. The police did not assert themselves unless they were confronted with especially grave transgressions, such as theft. The guilty were confined to a cell in the center of the camp. But at Compiègne organized pillage did not exist in the sense that it would be exercised by the Mafia of the concentration camps.

Thus our impression upon arrival was excellent. We again found fresh air, sunshine, and all sorts of distractions. Life was beautiful! Our impression was confirmed when our first soup was brought to us: the quality was good, but the quantity, a liter, astonished us. In addition, we received three hundred grams of bread and a spoonful of jelly or butter.

The camp itself was divided into three subcamps: Camp A, in which we lived; Camp B, reserved for English and American civilian prisoners; and Camp C, which at first was reserved for undesirables, and which later also housed new arrivals when the newcomers exceeded the number who could be accommodated in Camp A.

The population of our camp was heterogeneous. In general, the inmates could be classified in three categories. First, there were those convicted under common law, most of whom had served their term in prison and had been released to the Germans; there were the light-fingered gentlemen of Marseille, rounded up when Vieux-Port, the old quarter, was evacuated; there were some Algerians, adventurous aliens whose visas had been canceled. Most of the inmates seemed to be professional freeloaders to be scorned, and they remained rather negative toward any plan to promote social interaction.

Then there were the Communists, who were the best-organized group. They were also the group that had been in the camp the longest period of time. They were supportive of one another and practiced solidarity. They were consistent in their interpersonal relationships and animated by their great commitment to the struggle for their ideal and against fascism.

Finally, there were prisoners of all ages and varied backgrounds who had been involved in guerrilla activities or who had been suspected of such involvement. There were young people who had been arrested at the border, those who had been in the guerrilla forces, and some who had been apprehended for spying. In addition, there were older prisoners—industrialists, writers, teachers, movie actors, radio announcers, anybody who had held a professional position. Certain prisoners, such as Michel Clemenceau and Master Henri Teitgen, the father of my former professor, exerted an uncontested influence. The active and the reserve officers organized. This group and the Communist cell promoted camp order.

Thus hundreds of people, very different in class, education, and ideology, were united in the true solidarity of a common fate. And, because it was ever necessary to protect ourselves from undesirable elements, this microcosm of the French community fragmented into small, closed groups that ignored each other.

In spite of the favorable impression and the easing of tensions experienced upon arrival, the first two weeks presented hardships. Was it the open air? We were extremely hungry—to the point of not being able to think about anything else. We were preoccupied with our hunger. Near the kitchen we found some carrot tops; raw or cooked, they are not significantly nutritious. I must tell you that the prisoners devised a rather crafty culinary system. We had neither stove nor wood, but we boiled water by electrolysis. We needed only a can or, better yet, a bucket, and an electric wire with one end plugged in and the other end dropped into the water. Our technique for boiling water taxed the overloaded electric lines. We risked setting our wooden barracks on fire. The Germans frequently made surprise inspections and confiscated everything that we did not have time to camouflage. However, we always found a way to fabricate new material.

Demaison tried to persuade us to gather the young greens that came up with the grass. We recovered some peas from the dishwater thrown out of the kitchens. To eat, to eat, to eat—it was our only thought. There was in fact a canteen in the camp, but it was meagerly stocked with a pepper substitute and with toothpaste. Twice a week it was stocked with vegetables; when they were divided among all of us, they constituted a weak supplement to our daily diet, and the costs were prohibitive. There were some traffickers who must have earned their bread and butter by fixing such exorbitant prices, or did only the Germans reap the profit?

Since we were allowed a specific quantity of tobacco in the camp, we could raise money by selling our ration. A *Gauloise*—the unit of exchange—was worth ten to fifteen francs, depending on the fluctuations of supply and demand.

As soon as we arrived in the camp, we were accosted by individuals offering, for a price, to sneak our mail out of the camp. Each had connections more reliable than the others, and if we had allowed ourselves to be deceived by these con artists, we would have been robbed not only of our money but also of our hope. It is true that every day dozens of letters probably succeeded in leaving the camp, either with the few workers who left each morning to work on the outside or in the carts of the vegetable merchants or with the visitors. (After six months of detention, we had a right to a ten-minute visit!) Another postal system consisted of tying the letter to a stone to be thrown at night over the barbed wire to the road; the civilians who found it would take it upon themselves to mail it—but the approaches to the camp were not a boulevard! We threw so many dreams and illusions over the barbed wire that the Germans were obliged to clean up the papers. Nevertheless, one of my missiles succeeded in reaching its destination, and my aunts in Nîmes finally learned where I had been since my arrest in the Pyrenees. On July 25, while many others were still totally cut off from their loved ones, with trembling hands I unsealed my first letter and opened a package prepared with love.

From our original group of those taken prisoner at the border, six of us ate together and agreed to share all packages that we received. We consistently honored our agreement. At fairly regular intervals one or the other of us received a package; therefore, we regained strength. Furthermore, the Red Cross made a commendable effort to supplement camp provisions.

Once the problem of hunger became less poignant, we participated in sports for recreation and health. Our camp was admirably well equipped, for, as a former military camp, it boasted soccer fields, basketball and volleyball courts, and a track. We often played volleyball. Thanks to some professionals, some competent soccer teams were formed. The games promoted team spirit in the camp.

A theater committee, directed by actors, presented each Sunday afternoon a recreational performance in a barrack, "The Little Casino," reserved for this purpose. Anybody could participate, and some would-be actors spent the whole week in preparing a performance for the following Sunday. Songs, music, sketches, impersonations, games, and anecdotes delighted the whole camp; sometimes even our guards might be heard laughing reluctantly. Even a large fair was organized for August 15, 1943. From early in the morning, the lawn was covered with outlandish tents, erected of bedsteads and covers, which housed the most diverse attractions. Their imagination and ingenuity enabled the prisoners to create something from nothing.

But our activities at Compiègne were not limited to eating and playing. Thanks to significant donations of books from the Red Cross and the YMCA, a well-supplied library was established. I availed myself of it. The library, although of special interest to the students, was also used by others who wanted to learn. It goes without saying that a book provides great opportunity for escape.

The most memorable of our activities was of an intellectual order. Courses for small groups and for large groups were offered each day. Publicized well in advance, seminars on the greatest variety of subjects enjoyed wide popularity. Master Teitgen held us in the spell of his compelling oratorical power. I remember one lecture on the role of the lawyer that we acclaimed in an interminable standing ovation. Among us were those who had traveled extensively, read widely, learned much, and who shared their knowledge with others.

We could not know that these were the beautiful days of our captivity. How many times, later on, far from our native country, did we recall Compiègne with nostalgia.

But, for me, most precious at Compiègne was the community of faith and hope grouped around Pastor Marcel Heuzé of Marseille. Several months earlier, lodging during a conference had been provided for me in the home of Madame Heuzé after her husband had already been arrested. She did not doubt that I would soon join him. The beaming personality and the serene strength of Pastor Heuzé drew at least thirty zealous Protestants to him, but he knew so well how to make himself appreciated by everyone that several Catholics and agnostics also sought him out. Of course, in the deprivation of captivity, barriers are indeed relative. A room was assigned to us as a chapel. We could meet there any hour of the day, whenever we needed solitude—a remarkable privilege in a prison camp. The liturgical decor was very simple: a table on which stood a cross made in the camp and an open Bible; on the walls, two pencil inscriptions—"God is love" and "I am the Good Shepherd"; and some benches. The furnishings were adequate.

On Sunday morning a worship service was held, which a German officer usually attended. Monsieur Heuzé, obliged to write on scraps of paper salvaged from the wrappings of packages, was required to have his sermon approved by the camp commandant. Every morning at nine o'clock, those who wished to participate gathered for a short Bible reading, meditation, and prayer. We tried to discern God's will for our lives. The zeal and sincerity of these meetings seemed to make us receptive to the actual presence of Christ. We gained in our community of faith the reserve of strength that would sustain us when the frightening darkness would fall.

Every evening in our room, a Bible study was held that would attract as many as one hundred auditors. Monsieur Heuzé summarized alternately Old and New Testament books. He explained them clearly with extensive interpretations, emphasizing the unity of biblical inspiration and the message of salvation and redemption. For many, this message was new, and numerous discussions followed. God's word does not return to Him void.

The high point of our spiritual life was without doubt the Sunday evening sacrament of communion, which united us around the bread and the wine, commemorating until He comes the death of our Lord. We forgot the barbed wire. The noise of the boots faded away. Recalling the suffering of Christ, His path of sorrow, which is the path of all mortals, and His cross, we were called to a total reconsecration of our lives to Him Who had redeemed us. What a moment of adoration and joy we experienced as the pastor offered us the elements! "Come. All things are ready," he told us, and added, "This is my body which is broken for you. This is my blood which is shed for you."

Nobody can explain grace; nobody can explain the mystery of the incarnation. We accept it and we live by it.

Thus our days were filled with varied culinary, athletic, theatrical, intellectual, and spiritual activities; sometimes we were obliged to respond to an invitation: "I don't have the time!" We slept well in spite of the fleas.

At night, the rays of the searchlights untiringly swept the camp.

Sometimes a machine gun sounded as an escape attempt was aborted in blood. Several prisoners tried to cross the network of barbed wire at night; few succeeded. The most clever escape took place before our arrival. The prisoners crawled through an underground tunnel extending from beneath the barrack floor to the field on the other side of the barbed wire. To dig such a long tunnel presents serious difficulties. As the work progresses, it is necessary to shore up, to ventilate, to illuminate, and above all to dispose of the removed soil. Night and day, by relays the prisoners had worked at the project until it was completed. Those who helped were allowed to use the tunnel. But, if one attempt succeeded, how many failed, betrayed by informers, often at the last moment? Each of us dreamed of escape, and we proposed audacious plans, always unrealistic.

Once a week we were allowed to send special postcards that were issued to us. I always wrote the same sentences: "My morale is excellent. I am very touched by all that you have done for me. We have everything here except freedom. We shall see each other again soon." To tell the truth, we had nothing there because we did not have freedom. However, in contrast with what was to come, the time spent at Compiègne was a time of peace and enrichment. It was the calm before the storm.

For hours at a time I felt inclined to stretch out on the grass and to contemplate the heavens, the ever-moving Ile-de-France skies in ever-changing pastel hues. The clouds had never before appeared so beautiful. They corresponded to our mood, these light skies that bore the fleeting images of our dreams. We did not know yet that the skies of Germany would be always gray, a dirty and monotonous gray, reflecting the sadness of the earth.

From time to time the question of transfer was raised. One day, a convoy of Jews was formed for Drancy. We were ordered to form long lines, by barracks, and, proof in hand, to indicate whether or not we were Jews, we were required to march before the German inspector. How beastly! I can still see a sedate, bearded, orthodox priest holding his cassock over his arm. The System thrived on the humiliation of the individual. Our block leader, an amiable Protestant, was placed in the Jewish convoy only because he had been circumcised for medical reasons.

Our time came also. The evening of September 2, 1943, twelve hundred of us were detained after roll call. Suddenly, the atmosphere became electrified and our guards became nervous as if something were in the air. Each carrying a small bundle of his few treasures, we were quartered in an isolated barrack for the night. At the break of day, each of us was given a round of bread and a large sausage, and we formed ranks to leave the camp. Alas! The SS death's-head squads took charge with an impressive display of automatic weapons. We were marched through the city. Here and there, some wife or mother tried to see her loved one for the last time, but the police restrained the crowd that assembled along our route. The scene was anguishing. Before these unhappy but proud and fervent faces, we wanted to cry out: "Thank you! Thank you, people of Compiègne, for the strength that is in you and that shines in your faces. Thank you, people of France, who love us in spite of everything and for whom we will survive!"

By groups of sixty we were herded into cattle cars built to accommodate forty persons or eight horses. Packed like sardines in a can, we hardly had room to sit. A little straw and the inevitable bucket were thrown inside, and our doors were barred. Under the straw we found a chisel, hidden there no doubt by some worker. We learned later that such a tool had been concealed in each car: a sign of vigilante resistance on the part of the railroad workers.

As soon as our convoy was under way, one comrade began cutting around some screws in a board at the bottom of the back wall. He was a connoisseur; he took his time, but at last he loosened a plank to provide an adequate opening. Since the train traveled at high speed, we decided not to try to escape until the train would pull out of some station after nightfall. Some comrades, seized by fear, vehemently took us to task and threatened to alert the SS. All arguments were in vain. They were afraid of reprisals, and their fear dominated them. We were forced to threaten them in order to silence them. Very promising!

Alas! Our plans were nullified by the speed of the train as it crossed the border. We wanted to make our escape in France. At nightfall, we entered Saarbrücken, and to add insult to injury, the guards inspected the train and discovered the opening in our car. We were not the first to have attempted escape! A guard opened the door of our car and threatened us. He ordered us to take off our shoes, which were thrown into another freight car, and he herded at least fifty more prisoners into our already crowded car. Then a thick plank was nailed over the outside of the opening that we had made. Not only did our hopes take flight, but the journey itself now became a corporal punishment. We were so crowded that we could not move to attend to our physical needs or to try to breathe fresh air from the cracks between the boards.

Without food, without water, we traveled for three days. Several prisoners had used the tools to cut holes in the cars; not many suspected that a machine gun had been mounted on the caboose. Those daring few whom the speed of the convoy did not deter from slipping onto the roadbed were gunned down. From under our car came a scream of pain, and we knew that someone had fallen beneath the wheels; a second later, tac-tac-tac-tac-tac, then silence, and the nightmare passed into the darkness. How many succeeded in escaping? Surely very, very few. Upon arrival, the guards counted one hundred and eighty who had died or escaped.

Our legs and our backs were cramped. Thirst tormented us. When the train stopped in the stations, we cried out, "Something to drink, for pity's sake." But no one took pity on us, and our guards came to curse us through the cracks of our wooden walls. Those who could peer through the crevices saw an inhospitable land: beet fields and potato fields stretching out of sight, stations filled with uniformed personnel, columns of prisoners working along the rails, villages painted in bright colors, and many children. And everywhere the detested uniforms. We were on enemy territory.

There was a long stop. Then we were shifted into a freight station of which we read the name in gothic letters—Weimar. Some of us knew only that Weimar had once been the seat of a republic.

Buchenwald, the Gates of Hell

> It is through the grace of God that you are one who suffers rather than one who inflicts suffering.
>
> —Roland de Pury, *Living Stones*
> (Written in a cell at Montluc)

"Hurry up! Out! Out!" Abruptly the car doors were flung open; hoarsely bellowed commands reinforced by kicks of heavy boots launched us pell-mell onto the railroad embankment. Sprained ankles, our few remaining possessions lost in the confusion, no time to think! "Out! Out!" We could now well imagine what awaited us.

We were ordered to line up five abreast. We stood there on the freight station platforms until late afternoon. The SS guarded us with an evil eye and a finger on the trigger. Good heavens, what did they fear? We were all barefoot. Our shoes had been taken away to prevent escape attempts. Some prisoners indeed had been ordered to undress completely except for undershorts or a shirt or simply a jacket.

Shortly before nightfall we moved out from the station. Half-naked, we were marched through Weimar. Shamelessly, sneering maliciously, women with children gathered to watch us pass. Just think of it: French terrorists—what a spectacle for the master race! Bicycling across our path, a Gretchen called to the guards, "Why don't you kill them all?" What a contrast between this cynical arrogance and the compassion of our French women!

We turned onto a beautiful road through the heart of a woods of tall, full-grown trees. Night fell. We plunged into the unknown. The rough language, the unusual hour of the march, the number of guns pointed at us made me think of the Katyn massacre that the newspapers had widely reported. Were we on our way to such a liquidation?

As darkness deepened, the SS became increasingly mad. They

29

drove us forward with hefty blows of their rifle butts. Forced to run, we stepped on the heels of those in front of us. Nevertheless, as we were driven forward, we supported those who collapsed. In order to avoid the blows, those who were on the outside tried to move into the middle. There was pushing; there were shouted curses. We were panic-stricken. Running barefoot over stones that fiercely lacerated our feet, we covered nine kilometers in less than an hour. This scene of collective madness, of the hysterical and fiendish conduct of our guards, took on dreadful proportions. I still hear it. I will always hear it—the barking of mad men that echoed a thousand times through the gloom of the German woods, "Move, move, faster, you French swine!" A pack of mad dogs drove a miserable human herd.

Finally a clearing, signs, barbed wire, a gate, and we passed inside the first camp fence. We saw large buildings, factory chimneys, the monumental entrance to the prison camp, and haughty SS caps. An officer counted us and we found ourselves in the large assembly area in the middle of the camp.

The stage was set. Helping the SS, some camp police, Germans in boots and uniforms who were nevertheless prisoners like us, shoved us into block formations. Behind us, from the entrance gate, powerful searchlights beamed. Before us lay a corpse with arms crossed. Elongated shadows extended to the outline of the barracks, barely visible through the haze. Physically exhausted from the journey, demoralized by the reception, we stood in deadly, anguished silence. The Reich received us and tried to break us. Nevertheless, we had to survive. We did not know what was awaiting us. However, we understood that we were condemned without mercy to an unequal struggle and that we must fight to the end because we were, if only in the shadows, witnesses for a just cause.

Always guarded by camp police armed with clubs, we were led to the shower house. Once again it was necessary to wait, standing without breaking rank. It was late, we were hungry, we were thirsty, it was beginning to rain; the line moved slowly. Finally about 2:00 A.M. it was my turn. Instantly all my clothes were taken from me; I was completely naked, and all hairy parts of my body were shorn with electric clippers. I was showered, sprayed with disinfectant, and dressed in odds and ends pulled at random from the clothing pile. My file was prepared. I received a number and found myself outside with my comrades, who were completely bewildered. Thenceforth, I was known only as prisoner 20-801. Thus the machinery of German organization dehumanized.

As a nervous reaction, we burst out laughing to see ourselves thus transformed into clowns. The shower had produced a refreshing effect. Nevertheless, we were still obliged to stand in line outside, to wait in a freezing fine rain that trickled over our shaved heads.

The camp police led us to our quarters, block 63, the quarantine block, isolated from the others by barbed wire. As we crossed the camp, the wooden shoes that had been issued to us stuck in the mud; there was no solution to the problem other than to go barefoot. We were astonished at the size of the camp. Again we had to wait outside. As the rain continued, we sank in the mire. Day broke reluctantly through the somber gray. The dampness chilled us to the bone. We were sad enough to cry. I remembered it was Sunday—my first day at Buchenwald—a somber Sunday!

We hoped that we would be able to rest once we had entered the block, but there was to be no rest before night. We spent the whole day answering roll calls. Our new masters, a German block leader and his fanatical Polish accomplices, those in charge of the barrack, seized every opportunity to demonstrate their authority. Although they were prisoners like us, they intimidated us as they distributed mess tins and food and assigned quarters. We were introduced to the *Schlag,* called "interpreter" by our masters; a rubber hose filled with lead, it inflicted great pain.

The block leader, happy to have us in his power, made a long harangue. He reminded us that we were only Frenchmen and that he would teach us German discipline. He introduced us to the camp rules and ordered us to learn the commands in German. Ten times, twenty times, he told us to fall in; he shouted "Mützen ab" and "Mützen auf" (take off your cap, put on your cap), and he trained us to follow other equally silly commands. We never responded quickly enough to satisfy him; but what could he expect from us, who were only scum?

Our clothes were soaked by the rain. We had no handkerchief; we had not even a string with which to tie up our trousers, and we had no socks. We were miserable.

Near the assembly yard and dominating the whole camp was a tall chimney, the bell tower of a new religion. At this place of holocaust, victims were sacrificed. The next day, when the chimney belched a heavy black smoke, our guards gleefully informed us that it was from the crematory. Thus, this acrid cloud, pervading the humid air as it floated over the camp, was all that was left of our comrades who had died in transport.

We were at the end of our strength, and our will was gone. Like my comrades, I was one of the flock, doing whatever the others did, trying to disappear in the crowd—a sheep among sheep. This day had broken me, and I experienced the despair of Good Friday: "My God, why hast Thou forsaken me?" Such was my defeat, my physical anguish, my panic before the hideous threat of nothingness. All my confidence dissipated; I was in a whirlpool fifty thousand fathoms deep, and I did not know how to swim!

How far we were from Compiègne! The only improvement the change had brought us was in the diet. Every day we received five hundred grams of bread with a stick of margarine and a ring of sausage, as well as a liter of fairly hearty soup. This abundance at the outset prompted some not to request packages from their families.

Our quarantine lasted two weeks. We were kept busy with all sorts of formalities. We were given several physicals; we were weighed and measured, x-rayed, vaccinated a dozen times—against what, I do not know! We filled out questionnaires. What purpose did the physicals serve, since everyone, without exception, would be sent to work? In addition, our political dossier was compiled: we were photographed with a large number across the chest, and we were asked endless questions, worded to harass. The whole process was completely meaningless, but the System was satisfied; it ground on, and we could die legally.

A priest from Lorraine, Father Georges, was appointed interpreter for our group because he spoke German fluently. Fortunately, his strong personality, expressed in his skillful defense of us, favorably influenced our block leader, a politician embittered by ten years of imprisonment. Our position improved, and Father Georges gradually assumed the leadership in our block.

Our transport group had been divided into two blocks with about five hundred in each. We slept stuffed into three-tiered wooden "boxes." We slithered into them—there was not enough room for us to sit up—and, lying on our sides, we were bricked one against the other. Although there were not enough blankets, we kept one another warm; but it was very difficult to sleep well in a fixed position. It seemed that whenever the camp was about to regurgitate prisoners, more than twice the number would be choked into the same space. The term "concentration camps" was not a metaphor. Overcrowding was the rule.

We were the second large convoy of Frenchmen to arrive at Buchenwald; the first group, given inmate numbers from 14,000, had arrived in June. Both groups would be decimated by the rigors of the coming winter of 1943–44.

Permission to correspond with our families, who must have become very anxious, was deferred. From Compiègne, a simple postcard had advised them that we were being transferred and that they should not send any more packages. Prisoners at Buchenwald were permitted to write one letter a month, and amazingly enough, in contrast to the strict limitations often imposed on prisoners of war, there was no official restraint on the number of packages or letters we were permitted to receive. Finally we were allowed to write a letter but only in the German language. Since very few could write German, our interpreter constructed acceptable sentence models.

Naturally, whatever we reported about our new life had to be decidedly inoffensive. By citing various biblical passages—for instance, Psalm 23 : 4—I tried to make implications. But how could anyone understand what was happening to us? Unfortunately, these letters never reached their destination. I was not permitted to write again until January 1944; before that date arrived, I could have died a hundred times. After they had received the letter from Compiègne at the end of September 1943, my family and friends had gained no information about me.

In quarantine, we were not forced to work, but our guards were not content to see us unoccupied. Therefore, they assigned us to carry stones—not a very taxing detail. A thousand prisoners, five abreast and at a snail's pace, were led to the quarry that was located a few hundred meters from the camp. Each of us was required to carry back a large stone. We completed—without shouts, without blows, without excitement—three or four trips a day. Later, we would remember this time as one of unique exception. However, these trips allowed us to discover what the quarry really was—the worst assignment at Buchenwald. The newcomers were trained in the quarry as soon as their quarantine ended. Also assigned to the quarry were those being punished and those whom the camp officials had marked for death. Now we saw with our own eyes what forced labor was. Camp police and foremen lashed with the *Schlag* miserable, striped phantoms, clinging to their pickaxes, to their shovels, to their stones. A heavy cart, to which were harnessed twenty groaning Russians, was toilsomely drawn up a steep bank. Only those imprisoned without hope of release understood the meaning of "Nazi labor camp."

The camp was hidden in a forest of beech trees (whence its name "Buchenwald") on a hill about six hundred meters high, overlooking the plain on which the city of Weimar is situated. The weather was mild in those days of mid-September, and the air was light. Unfortunately, Buchenwald is exposed to penetrating winds. At all seasons, the assembly yard was swept by a wind which drove before it rain, fog, or snow. Is it credible that such a location was consciously selected?

I used my free time during the quarantine to begin to learn German, which was to become very useful, for it was a great advantage to know what was being said and planned. The Germans did not tolerate our ignorance of their language, and they became enraged with those Frenchmen who could only respond, "Nix compris." It is understandable that in our position we had no particular love for these guttural sounds, and many of our comrades, even with sustained effort, could barely remember their inmate number. Their ineptitude earned them many extra slaps, punches, kicks, loss of rations, and because they failed to answer roll call, poor work assignments. In brief, ignorance of the language sometimes shortened their lives. In such a struggle, the player can never hold enough trumps.

Whenever there was any leisure time after the many roll calls and details, Albert and some other friends and I loved to meet for conversation. Our morale, so low on the Sunday of arrival, had revived. Despite hardships, we were acclimating. Because we could not change our situation, we simply sought to cling to life. We encouraged one another. Certainly the abrupt plunge into the world of a Nazi concentration camp was shocking. If we should survive this experience, we should never forget it! We could not conceive that the human heart could engender such hatred; we could not comprehend this sadistic pleasure that fed on the suffering of others. But if the SS were the prime promoters of hatred, they enlisted, through their terrorism, a few docile disciples among the prisoners willing to assist them. Those in positions of leadership were prisoners, most of whom had already spent years in concentration camps and had survived only because they had come to terms with the System. The main goal of the camp was to dehumanize us. The demoniac genius of the Nazi concentration camp regime lay in having placed us, its victims, in a relationship of hating each other.

From the beginning, we set ourselves against the Russians and the

Poles, whose instincts seemed primitive and brutal to us. In their defense, it must be said that they had witnessed much bestiality during the two or three years that they had been imprisoned. The following scene illustrates how they introduced us to the law of the underworld.

During a relatively peaceful afternoon, I heard prolonged wailing coming from the lavatory barrack. We had developed a certain insensitivity to the suffering of others, but these cries rent the soul, and I went to see what was happening. Many inmates had gathered to witness the summary execution of four German kapos, or chiefs. After an absence of several months, a work group, assigned to work outside of Buchenwald, had just returned to the camp, and the Russian members of the group were avenging themselves of the mistreatment inflicted by their kapos. The SS did not interfere because, once the group was dissolved, the kapos lost their privileges. These acts of revenge, although not openly encouraged, were inherent in the System that devoured its most "loyal" servants. What occurred was inconceivable. The Russians, armed with metal rods, had deliberately disemboweled their victims; when they lost consciousness, the Russians threw a bucket of cold water on the kapos to revive them so that their suffering could be extended. All afternoon they agonized, subjected to the taunts of their executioners, until death freed the fallen chiefs or until a physician inmate gave them a lethal injection. I quickly turned away from this nauseating horror scene, but the smell of blood and the butchers' gleeful exaltations remained with me for a long time.

Otherwise, our days dragged on monotonously. We knew nothing of our future except that we would probably be assigned to one of Buchenwald's extension camps. Some of the military news—that of the invasion of Italy and of Pietro Badoglio's successful coup against Mussolini—incited hope. All of us were convinced that the war could not continue much longer and that we would be home by Christmas. How could we have lived without hope? In the hour of deepest despair, we believed resolutely in ultimate Allied victory.

Our quarantine ended on September 18, and we moved to the main part of the camp. What an experience! We were assigned to block 31. Our first impressions were favorable. The blocks were clean, decorated with flowers, and divided into dormitories, mess halls, and toilets.

We became acquainted with the camp and with the people of various nationalities—mainly Russians, Poles, and Czechs. German political prisoners were in charge of most of the groups that worked under the Buchenwald administration. Therefore, these groups were better organized than were those that worked under extension camp administrations. Criminal offenders were in charge of the outside work groups, held under Mafia-like intimidation.

Each prisoner wore, sewn on the left side of his jacket and the right side of his trousers, his number and a triangle with the first letter of his nationality. The red triangle indicated political offender; green, criminal offender; black, saboteur; purple, Jehovah's Witness or other conscientious objector; pink, homosexual offender; yellow, Jew—rapidly disappearing!

We met some Frenchmen who had arrived in June and we bombarded them with questions. Most of them worked in an arms factory not far from the camp, and their living conditions at that moment were still tolerable. But the rumors they passed along about the work groups of the extension camps were not encouraging. The best assignments were to the Buchenwald work groups, but to procure such an assignment required the assistance of someone in the work-statistics office. Slim chance!

The camp itself, as seen by a visitor just passing through, was rather attractive. The blocks were built in a straight line, clean, surrounded by gardens; vases of flowers stood in the windows. Many small cities would have been proud of the layout, which provided a garden in which beautiful vegetables were grown, a model farm, a hospital, a movie theater, and even a brothel. Near the kitchens, the mighty oak under which Goethe once daydreamed was carefully preserved. Nothing that contributed to human happiness was lacking, not even German romanticism. But for those who experienced the reality, the picture changed dramatically. Ashes from the crematory fertilized the garden; in the brothel, reserved for the petty officers, the girls of the various nationalities were not volunteers but had been forcibly deported; in the hospital, in the blocks, and throughout the camp, how much physical and spiritual distress was experienced! Not the least of the paradoxes of the soul of our oppressors was that at the same time that they cultivated hatred, they cultivated flowers. Their malicious genius sneered as they listened to the sweetest harmonies, and they showed the deepest feelings for little birds but swatted men as if they were flies.

We were disquieted by the experimentation block, about which hushed rumors were circulated. No one knew exactly what was taking place there. Several rows of barbed wire fence isolated it from the other blocks. It was rumored that some prisoners were being used as guinea pigs for medical experiments. German physicians, held as prisoners, were employed there; there was an adjoining laboratory associated with scientific institutions and universities. Rarely did an inmate return from his stay in the medical block. What price scientific progress! The Hippocratic oath was thrown into the wastebasket of history!

Morning and evening, the several thousand prisoners were mustered in perfect formation in the assembly area where our infamous reception had taken place. At the command through the loudspeaker, "Mützen ab," all caps were removed with military precision. Roll call lasted about an hour, sometimes longer. All eyes sought the clock above the gate. At night eight searchlights blinded us. Roll call was especially debilitating in winter, when the temperature dropped to twenty degrees below zero (Celsius) and for hours we were required to stand in formation, feet in the snow, stomachs empty, shriveled by fatigue.

About six o'clock, when morning roll call was over, the work commandos were sent off to work by a trumpet fanfare. How can this absurd spectacle, which the guards seemed to take seriously, be portrayed? A circus orchestra, composed of prisoners costumed in red trousers and blue jackets with gold braid, heralded, with a rhythm that would have made bears dance, the departure of the work brigades. Was this spectacle created to illustrate one of the slogans of the Reich, "Work is pleasure"? Hypocrisy reached its full measure at Buchenwald!

As our first duty, we were assigned to the preferred task of what was called, as a euphemism, garden work. It was Sunday. All night it had rained torrents. The soaked ground was like wet clay. Various sorts of crates with long poles for carrying litter-fashion were distributed. In groups of two we were expected to fill the crates at the latrine and run with them five hundred meters back to the garden. The load was very heavy. We sank into the mud up to our calves. From the outset my wooden shoes were mud blocks, and I had to take them off, but then the stones gashed my feet. We had to work quickly. On the second trip, we slowed down. The kapo who was our guard, wearing a green triangle, began to scream like a madman. He lashed us with the *Schlag*. It began to rain again, and we could move only with the greatest difficulty through the mud. At last we literally sank up to our knees in the mire, and every effort to extricate a leg was exhausting. With no firm footing, we could hardly balance our precious cargo. The kapo yelled, "Move, move, I'll teach you, you dirty Frenchmen!" It rained even harder. We were wet through and through. Where could we find shelter? But our troubles were only beginning, for an SS guard, who wanted to demonstrate his savoir-faire, arrived with an enormous wolf dog. And he shouted, and he whipped, and he set the dog on our heels. The beast terrorized us, but we did not dare fall out of line. Some comrades had bleeding calves and torn trousers. In three assaults I felt fangs in my buttocks and in my calves. (These wounds festered and did not heal for several weeks.) When the kapo was at one end of the run, we relaxed our efforts at the opposite end; but he was quick to notice and with blows of his truncheon to set us in motion. The harassment lasted until evening. For me this same routine lasted three days, at the end of which, one morning, I persuaded my block chief to declare me unfit for work because my foot wounds had become infected. I had learned from experience what the labor camp was.

Shortly thereafter preparations were made to send us to another camp. The famous blue-and-gray striped pajamas were distributed (as a precaution against escape), and we did not work anymore while we were waiting for departure. This reprieve was welcomed. We benefited from it by learning about the barter system in the camp: a cigarette was worth fifty pfennige or twenty-five grams of margarine.

At this time another convoy, assigned inmate numbers from 21,000, arrived from Compiègne. Among the newcomers I discovered several friends, including Pastor Heuzé and André Guyonnaud, both very courageous men. The journey for this group had been very uncomfortable: the prisoners had been crowded beyond belief. When one of the cars, in which one hundred and thirty had been herded, was opened, eighty, dead of suffocation, tumbled out one over the other. There were continuous scenes of slaughter and of lunacy. No excuse can be offered for these crimes.

Finally a secretary from the work-statistics office announced the convoy list. As my number was called, I stepped forward. My wounds caused me to limp. Because able-bodied men were needed, the secretary struck my number from the list. I felt a sense of relief. However, I was to be separated from several comrades. Bound for Dora, most of them would die in the unbearable conditions of the winter of 1943–44.

Three days later, when my number was called, I did not escape. About two hundred of us were chosen to form a work brigade— Frenchmen, Russians, Poles, Czechs, and some Germans. After we had answered to several roll calls, we were loaded, with our indispensable mess tin, spoon, and two blankets, into a truck. These convoys were always an ordeal because the inmates were packed like sardines in a can. The Russians and the Poles harassed me. They all wanted to sit, and they bullied me because I was French. A kind of complicity always came into play against those who were weak and isolated. I stood on one leg for almost the entire trip.

We rolled along for several hours. We noticed the fields and forests. We knew nothing except that we were going to Laura, a growing extension camp, about which we had heard favorable reports.

It was October 1, 1943. For students, at home, a new school year was beginning. For us, a new forced labor assignment!

Laura, Extermination Camp

*At the precise moment of terror,
bereavement, or physical pain, you
may catch your man when his
reason is temporarily suspended.
But even then, if he applies to
Enemy headquarters, I have found
that the post is nearly always
defended.*

—C. S. Lewis,
The Screwtape Letters

We halted. The barbed wire told us that we had arrived at our destination. Despite our numbness, shouts that we were beginning to understand all too well urged us to jump quickly from the trucks. There we were, lined up between large slate-gray buildings. In our curiosity about the place where we were to live, we noticed little other than this slate landscape relieved only by a few birch trees sprinkled by a fine rain. This indescribably cold and depressing gray-on-gray specter was Laura, one of Buchenwald's extension camps.

Immediately we met Schmidt, the obese SS officer, who was waiting to receive us. Previously at Buchenwald he had been known for toying with his pistol whenever he inspected the quarry commando, and he had been nicknamed "The Killer." He was the one who took charge of us, counted us, and led us to our building.

We were lodged in an expansive, drafty shed where bedsteads had been set up on which straw mattresses had been placed. It was dark and very cold; we shivered all night.

We met Frenchmen who three weeks earlier had arrived in a convoy of three hundred prisoners from Buchenwald. We were eager to hear what they would tell us about the food and about the work. Since they had been among the first arrivals, they had been obliged to manage from nothing to set up camp, or something approaching one, in these vast, inhospitable sheds. Naturally, they were first ordered to string the barbed wire fences. The discipline that the SS imposed reflected a zealous determination to prevent escapes.

Overseeing the minutest details of camp organization, Schmidt was always at our heels. *Schlag* in hand, he was the uncontested master of the camp. All day long he ordered us to carry bedsteads, put mattresses in place, nail boards. In the evening, at roll call, the commandant, Blaue, wearing boots and gloves and always wielding a truncheon, made the usual welcoming speech: "Whoever will not work or whoever becomes ill will not eat. Whoever will not observe the discipline imposed by the SS and the kapos will be severely punished. Whoever steals or tries to escape, whoever is suspected of stealing or trying to escape, will be hanged." Fine outlook!

Before dawn the next morning after roll call, we were divided into work commandos. Most of the new arrivals were assigned to the Dany Commando, which was named for the corporation in charge of the slate quarry, and were sent to work there. Several small teams of masons, carpenters, and electricians were formed. These constituted the desirable commandos. I had the good fortune to be appointed to a commando assigned to prepare a permanent campsite in a nearby expropriated hamlet. The commando assignments, made by the camp prisoner-secretary, were based on the occupations which we had declared. For once our competencies were to be rationally employed! When we had arrived at Buchenwald, the old-timers had warned us under no circumstances to declare ourselves students, a status that would assure assignment to the quarry commandos in which the mortality rate was highest. The regime did not especially like intellectuals. I found it necessary to invent a manual skill. Thinking that painting was considered respectable in Germany, I declared myself a painter! Hardly a month passed in which we were not asked our occupation. I claimed in turn to be a farmer (thinking naïvely that I would be sent to a farm), an engineer, a painter, a mechanic, and an electrician. Finally, having exhausted these pretensions, I contented myself with "student" and put my fantasy to rest.

Indeed, at first, my occupational declaration did help. The camp secretary, in need of painters, summoned me, along with another Frenchman, to the work location. We were joined by a Russian locksmith and a Polish mason, and under the eye of a guard, we comprised a commando of painters assigned to renovate a villa acquired for the camp commandant. Ours was a truly fine commando. Our guard said nothing to us as he whiled away the time; no kapo or foreman supervised us. Protected from inclement weather, we worked under a civilian who, unfortunately, hardly understood us at all. The work was easy. Nevertheless, we had to pretend to know the trade if our ruse was to be successful. I was embarrassed when I was instructed to remove the wallpaper, which was impervious to scraper and sponge. I tried to explain that in France we use other methods and other tools. Fortunately, I was not rushed. I suspected the Russian and the Pole of trying to discredit us and of conspiring to have us replaced by their compatriots. The villa overlooked the countryside, and we could view from our location the vast circle of the slate quarry in which our comrades worked. We could see them, like innumerable lines of little ants, busy with tip trucks all day long, pushing them, emptying them, filling them, and beginning again, without end.

In the camp, the law of the jungle prevailed. When food was distributed, the Russians, in particular, stormed the soup kettles and the bread supplies, and there was never enough for everybody. Sometimes, to disperse the horde of savages, the one distributing the food would strike out with a club or even a soup-filled dipper. Blankets, mattresses, mess tins, and shoes disappeared while prisoners slept; every item was subject to theft. It was necessary to fight to protect ourselves and to regain those possessions upon which life itself depended, for without mess tins there would be no soup and without shoes our feet would be torn by the sharp slate.

After a few days, a boil appeared on my left ankle and caused excruciating pain. My leg swelled, and I could walk only with difficulty. A very rudimentary infirmary, staffed by a German, a Czech, and two Poles, had been set up in one of the sheds. I went there for help. Fortunately, the Czech understood me; having been a student at Montpellier and in Paris, he spoke French. He was Georges Klouda, a lawyer from Prague. A very sympathetic person, he rendered great service to the French, but since he had little other than iodine and Band-Aids at his disposal, he could not perform miracles. The next day I dragged an elephantesque leg. The kapo in charge of the infirmary agreed to assign me a bed there and to excuse me from work.

Thus I took up residence in what served as an infirmary. No farmer concerned with protecting his investment would have raised hogs there! It was a kind of cellar—low, without either fresh air or light—furnished with about ten beds. Already admitted were a patient whose leg had been crushed by a tip truck, a tubercular patient, one with rheumatism, and several with infections similar to mine. In a corner was the sanitary bucket, seldom emptied, sometimes overflowing, turning the earthen floor to mire. The filth was repulsive; used bandages, mucus, and a nauseating odor of pus and of excrement were everywhere.

I spent ten days cloistered in this hovel while my leg oozed copiously. The kapo lanced the boil with his scalpel. Of course, he gave me no anesthesia. For a week, I was obliged to use the same paper bandage. When it was finally removed, there was an intolerable stench. The gaping, inflamed wound made me apprehensive that my leg was gangrenous and that it might be necessary to amputate it. I was suffering, but it was, nevertheless, a relief to stretch out on a mattress, even in this sewer, and to escape work, roll call, and the special details of every description. Our meals—one liter of soup, one slice of bread and margarine, just enough to keep us alive while we were not working—were brought to our bedside. During the day, we seldom saw the infirmary staff. Medicines were so limited that healing depended on nature, fortified by a strong will. Survival of the fittest!

Another convoy arrived from Buchenwald. To my great satisfaction, Albert was among the new arrivals. He visited me in the infirmary. His presence was a great comfort to me. I felt less alone.

As the number of sick and injured increased each day, I was obliged to relinquish my place, and the clinic kapo discharged me from the infirmary. I was assigned to the Dany Commando. We were required to work like beasts to haul the loaded tip trucks and to push them up a slope in order to dump the slate into a ravine. An evil little kapo struck us each time we raised our heads or paused for a minute. We worked twelve hours a day. I was broken by fatigue, and my arm and leg muscles knotted; the boil reopened, and I dragged a leg of lead. My plight evoked no indulgence from the kapo—far from it. This was a labor camp!

On the third day, due to the condition of my leg, I was sent back to the infirmary, where I was allowed to remain in bed for four days; but I needed at least a month of complete rest. During this time, about one hundred Italian soldiers from Badoglio's army arrived. First the SS and then the Russians robbed them. They were issued the prisoner's striped uniform; eight days later their military uniforms were returned to them. (The return of the uniforms was the only formal recognition of the Geneva Convention regarding the treatment of prisoners of war.) Poor, defenseless fellows, Neapolitans more adept at playing the guitar than at wielding a pickax, they were despised and mistreated. One of them, a victim of malaria, was brought to the infirmary soon after his arrival. After three days he died, gesticulating wildly and never ceasing in his lament, "Mama, mama mia!" A few hours later, a twenty-year-old Basque followed him in death. The cutting-off of young lives had begun.

Time passed slowly, very slowly in the infirmary. Fortunately, my neighbor was a young Breton with whom I could discuss many subjects: his province, his studies, our plans. Military news especially interested us, for we felt that our days here were numbered. Had not

Churchill predicted great events before autumn? The rumor spread that the Allies had landed at Marseille and Toulon and were rapidly advancing up the Rhone Valley; some rumors had it that Paris had already been reached. We no longer doubted that we would be home for Christmas.

I could not be kept in the infirmary indefinitely, even though my leg was not yet healed. Fortunately, I was admitted to convalescence. Thus, while my comrades were working themselves to death from morning till night, about twenty of us who were disabled were permitted to remain in the camp. Theoretically, we could not work, but Schmidt always found some task we could perform. He also conceived the perverse idea of withholding half the bread ration from the sick. Therefore, for almost a month, I received only two hundred and fifty grams of heavy war bread—a very small amount; but I preferred restricted rations to work in the quarry.

In the evening my comrades returned absolutely exhausted. No one knew exactly what was being planned for this quarry, but obviously the Germans attached importance to the project. Sometimes civilians or military officers were driven to the quarry to inspect the sites. Our masters seemed upset that the work did not progress quickly enough. It was necessary to clear a wide area where a railroad was to be laid next to the quarry; therefore, we were obliged to remove a mountain of stones and rocks that had been accumulating, no doubt, for generations. The discipline was murderous; we were forbidden to raise our head, to sit, to speak, to smoke, to catch our breath, even for a minute. The *Schlag* fell without mercy and kept everyone bent over his stones. Hunger tormented us, our faces were drawn, our shoulders drooped.

The quarry site was frightfully bare and forlorn. It was an immense circle, hewn in ledges to facilitate the extraction of the slate. Here and there were some gaunt birch trees. This slate circle limited our horizon. We knew that we were in Thuringia, several kilometers from a village called Lehesten and about eighty kilometers from the Czech border. We felt that we were light-years away from any civilization! It was a scorched earth, this land of forced labor. And we had only begun the ascent of Calvary, the Calvary of forced labor, which we would be forced to climb to the summit. But how many would reach that summit? Among the French there were many young students who had not yet attained physical maturity, and their bodies were not conditioned for such duress. Already, for those not accustomed to handling the shovel and the pickax for twelve hours a day, the ordeal had become exhausting. Those under eighteen (and there were some) and those over fifty were most vulnerable. Among those in the prime of life, some had arrived at the camp already weakened by long prison terms and by the tortures inflicted by the Gestapo. The Poles and the Russians seemed more durable, at least those with whom we came into contact. They had already survived the rigors of two winters. But the Poles and Russians did not hesitate to engage in treacherous activity. Emboldened by their numbers and solidarity, they always managed to relegate to us the least desirable assignments. Furthermore, some of them, able to make themselves understood by the Germans, did not hesitate to spy. There were of course exceptions, excellent comrades; but, in general, these Slavs had become contaminated by the System. The arrival of the Italians also caused complications. These prisoners naïvely believed that they could ingratiate themselves with the Germans by excessive zeal and dramatic flair. The only result was to incite the SS against the other inmates, sluggards by contrast. With the coming of the first cold days, the Italians, their energy already spent, died like flies.

By a caprice of nature, the end of October was like late summer. One Russian, taking advantage of the fine weather, escaped. In spite of the number of sentries, it was relatively easy to clear the quarry. But in his striped uniform, where could an escapee go, lost in this country, not knowing the language, without money, without durable shoes, without provisions? In the evening, at roll call, which as punishment lasted until midnight, the alarm was sounded. The manhunt in the surrounding countryside began with dogs. At the end of three days, the man was brought back to the camp; he was beaten unmercifully, then tied for three days to a tree in the camp—for three days, unable to move from the spot for any reason whatsoever! A large red circle was sewn on the back of his jacket and on the side of his trousers. This infamous target marked him for the vindictiveness of the SS. After he was sent back to work, he did not escape even one fatigue duty until one day a shot liberated him from his dog's life.

We were serving an apprenticeship in the savage struggle for survival. It was necessary to be on guard constantly and to defend ourselves. Theft was the general rule, and we were surrounded by professional thieves. If we took off our shoes and jacket at night, it was necessary to sleep on them, and still it was not uncommon, upon awakening, to find them gone. When another convoy, which brought the camp population to a thousand, arrived, there were not enough beds. Mattresses and blankets were stolen. Although we desperately needed our rest, we were never certain of finding a corner in which to stretch out for a few hours. We were forced to "organize"—as the prisoners say in camp jargon—to fight to recover and to fight to retain what we had recovered; otherwise, we would have been forced to sleep on the damp, cold ground. Every day, morning and evening, the same battles were repeated.

Each soup distribution became a chore. We were required to stand in line to be served and sometimes had to wait half an hour or three-quarters of an hour. Nobody wanted to wait his turn. There was seldom enough soup left to serve the last in line. Schmidt was often present to police us in his fashion; he struck with brutal force those who were shoving, or he turned the water hose on them.

We never assembled quickly enough to satisfy Schmidt. At the sound of his whistle, everyone had to run to the yard. There were nearly a thousand prisoners in the shed, and all of us had to pass through one narrow door at which, truncheon in hand, he waited for us. We pushed each other; the human wave surged against the bottleneck, and there were few who could avoid the *Schlag*. The blows were threatening. All those in charge, from the SS to the kapos, relied upon the *Schlag*.

When we returned, exhausted from work, we were forced to compete aggressively for everything; and to refuse to fight was to be defeated in advance. In order to avoid the *Schlag* and special work details, we stood impassively throughout roll call, and we learned not to call attention to ourselves. There was not a moment of rest, of peace, or of conversation with the friends whom we had met; we were always tense and on the alert. Even at night, our sleep was interrupted every two hours by the arrival and departure of the night shifts. Yes, there were night shifts so that the work of excavating the shafts in the mine would not be interrupted.

Thus October passed. There were not many deaths, but all of our comrades were exhausted, and winter had not yet begun.

I was still in convalescence because my leg remained infected. Glad to avoid the strenuous commando work, I was not eager for my leg to heal. But Schmidt, who was tired of seeing me remain inactive, found in an "easy" commando a task I could perform while seated. With several others, I peeled potatoes in a room near the kitchen twelve hours a day. The assignment was certainly not desirable—the quota was demanding, and a kapo harassed us continuously—but the work was infinitely more pleasant than was breaking stones, and sometimes we received a little extra soup.

At the end of October, the permanent camp in the hamlet on the hill was finished, and on the evening of November 1, 1943, we moved there.

The first impression was excellent because, instead of dirty sheds, we now had respectable buildings. An unbroken ring of electrified barbed wire marked the perimeter of the camp. The old farm buildings had been arranged in three blocks; in addition, there were the kitchen, the assembly yard, of course, and even a lawn. The potato-peeler commando was quartered in a room in block 2. We were lucky, since the other blocks housed mainly large dormitories and the few smaller rooms were reserved for German personnel.

Thus I spent my time peeling potatoes while my leg continued to cause me pain. Suddenly, during roll call on November 3, the sky darkened, the temperature dropped as if chilled by a current from the Siberian Steppes, and the first snowflakes flurried. We shivered in our thin, striped clothing. How would we survive a winter that was arriving so prematurely?

The next day I was again admitted to the infirmary. This time it was not the infamous stable of the old camp. I spent nine days in a comfortable, warm bed, and I infinitely appreciated this unheard-of luxury. However, I could not help but think of my comrades who slaved all day in the quarry, many of whom were already alarmingly emaciated.

Those few days in the infirmary provided for such an oasis of peace and rest that I could only give thanks to Him who holds my life in His hand. This respite gave me time to seek communion with Him, which is not possible when the body is broken by fatigue and the spirit is annihilated. In intercession I brought before Him my loved ones in France, with their difficulties and anxieties. We must believe that we are faithfully sustained. This belief is the foundation of our existence. I do not know why just at that time God was confirming the call to the ministry I had received a short time before my arrest. If God willed, I would return and I would consecrate myself to the dissemination of His word. I believe that I can say with certainty that even in the time of greatest trial when fear threatened to exterminate all hope, this conviction never left me.

In the morning on November 6, upon awakening, I noticed that snow had fallen heavily during the night and had covered everything. Under other circumstances, this wintry beauty would have enchanted me; but here, the struggle for survival caused me to dread the additional hardships that the cold would impose. General Winter did not fight on our side. The snow would not melt until the end of April. There would be six months during which we would see only wet or frozen ground and a cloudy sky resolutely closing out the sun, six months of desolation and of death. Laura, land of forced labor!

On November 12, I could no longer be accommodated in the infirmary; there were too many who were ill. But I was admitted to convalescence for a stay that would be prolonged until December 20. On this date, once again, I would share the hard work of the commandos. My leg was still in unsatisfactory condition, but it would heal in January. The leg infection had saved my life. Thanks to this infection, I was excused from harder labor for two and one-half months and was sheltered from the cold and the inclemencies that caused the high mortality rate among my comrades.

The convalescence ward accommodated quite a few people, even though Schmidt mercilessly sent most of the sick to work. Actually three-fourths of the prisoners in the camp had already been ill and needed an extended rest. Of this number, some were definitely unable to work, but the total number in the infirmary or in convalescence was not permitted to exceed 10 percent of the camp population. This was the rule. When it was acknowledged that a prisoner was ill, his admittance to the infirmary or to the convalescence ward was at the expense of another, who, sick or well, had to move out. This struggle for a place in the clinics provoked daily conflicts.

During the day, those convalescing were assembled in a room in block 2. The ward was a waiting room for miraculous healing. Patients suffered from the most diverse afflictions: some, living skeletons, no longer had the strength to move; others, swollen by edema or tortured by infections, hardly fared better; some were wasting away with dysentery, while still others, racked by tuberculosis, were spitting out their lungs.

All of these patients occupied a room that served as a dormitory at night. A fetid odor of pus, of excrement, of infected lungs hovered there; the floor was strewn with bloody balls of mucus and with discarded bandages. The room was dark and poorly ventilated. It was necessary to have a strong stomach in order not to become nauseated from the stench. In this place, the seriously ill died; the healthier patients became seriously ill.

When our comrades returned from work, nothing was more demoralizing for them than the sight of the convalescent ward. Often, they had to remove from his bed some poor devil who had just drawn his last breath. All too frequently, they had to pull from the table a fellow inmate leaning on elbows rigid in eternal sleep. Daily, they had to step over corpses stretched out on the floor and remove them from the ward. The dead were everywhere. They were found in every corner—on the assembly yard, in the blocks, in the toilets, in the infirmary. Everywhere the living must move the dead in order to make room for those still clinging to life. We fought not so much for life as against death, against the dead, against death's invasion of the camp. The battle was unending.

Murderous for all of us, but especially for the ill, was the roll call. It could last several hours twice a day—before the departure for work and after the return. All except those confined to the infirmary were required to report. It was not unusual that a corpse, not yet officially dead, was dragged into ranks at roll call. Once the SS ordered that a corpse be carried to the quarry; at roll call the prisoner had been counted in the commando, and upon return he would have to be counted again. Naturally, such callous and brutal orders were given to destroy our morale. We wished that our masters would at least let us die in peace, but the SS only mocked and derided the dying who fell at their feet. Paleontologists tell us that care for the dead is one of the characteristics that distinguishes man from animal! Was not this attempt to kill not only the body but also the soul a satanic endeavor?

Roll call was all the more appalling because of the freezing temperatures that had set in. We suffered from the cold at work also, but there we were moving. At roll call we were required to stand still. We could not feel our feet or our fingers; our shoulders became brittle, and the numbness spread. We were too undernourished to generate any significant body heat. It would have been so satisfying to lie down in the snow and to sleep, to sleep. And what could we do when we had dysentery and could not control an irrepressible urge; how could we avoid the frightful beatings we received when we had to relieve ourselves? Frequently, when roll call ended and the columns marched away, we saw four or five prisoners stretched on the ground, faces in the snow, dead or dying.

These first cold spells claimed a large number of our young compatriots, those in their twenties, weakened by lack of food, exhausting work, beatings, and insufficient sleep. Both pneumonia and dysentery spread rampantly because of the crowded conditions and poor hygiene.

My friend Jean Durand became seriously ill with the grippe, accompanied by a violent fever. In the quarry he worked in the most demanding commando, unsheltered from the wind. One day in November, after a visit to the infirmary, it was recognized that he was ill. He was given two aspirin tablets and admitted to convalescence. We met in the convalescent ward. A few minutes later the SS arrived to check the patients. Durand's temperature was taken. Since the aspirin had reduced his fever, he was released without any further instructions, and the same night he was ordered back to work with his commando. For twelve hours of excavation work on the night shift, he was unsheltered from the icy winds. Shivering with fever that had seized him again, he was too weak to raise his pick or to lift the stones. All night he was mercilessly beaten by Jupp, a dreaded German kapo with a deformed neck, who wore the red triangle. The next morning my poor Jean was carried back by four comrades, and he died several hours later, his body black and blue and covered with welts. Thus a robust young man of twenty-six years, a junior officer, was beaten to death. There had been a bond between us because, like me, he was from Tirman, a small village of the Algerian high plateaus. Ah! He who in such moments does not feel a desire for vengeance is not normal! How could I forgive? Is it possible that Jean's murderer did not know what he was doing? Was there not satanic vision in the brutality? Is hatred not blinding? Perhaps it would have been easier to forgive what I suffered than to forgive what my comrades suffered and what I cannot forgive in their place. More than once we were on the verge of taking revenge, but such an attempt would have been folly. We could only clench our fists in silence; we had to satisfy ourselves with the conviction that such crimes would ultimately be avenged.

The atmosphere of the convalescent ward was depressing; it was a little antechamber of the crematory. If we were sick enough to be admitted, we were too sick to have much chance of recovery. Nevertheless, the convalescent ward offered comparative repose and was for most of us our best hope for survival. But accommodations were limited and few of us were admitted; the Germans and the Poles were given preference over the "inferior races."

My Czech attendant Georges Klouda, a lawyer from Prague and a former secretary to President Beneš, did what he could with the little that he had. Since he needed an aid, he arranged for me to be assigned as an attendant in the infirmary. Thus for two weeks I helped, especially with the cleaning chores. There were so many duties that there was no free time, but the infirmary was preferable to the convalescent ward. Furthermore, I felt that I was being useful. It was difficult to keep the room spotless, even though there were only about twenty beds. Edouard, a nineteen-year-old from Bordeaux, kept me busy. He had dysentery, and I had to bathe him with a soapless, wet cloth every day. If I had not bathed him, he would have died in the filth. This poor boy could no longer eat or drink; at the end of ten days, he succumbed to his illness, and death put an end to his suffering. In undressing him, for it was necessary to return all clothes to the camp administration, I found a letter from his mother. He was her only son. "My dear, what has become of you? Are you cold and hungry? I am so alone without you." Oh! The sadness of mothers! Is man born only to suffer?

I was in charge of undressing the dead, all of whom were brought to the infirmary. At that time, out of a thousand prisoners, six or seven corpses were brought to the infirmary each day; later, the number increased. At first I did not like my job, but then one adapts; one adapts to anything! Some of the bodies were mere skeletons, and it seemed to me that they would break in half as I undressed them; others were bloated, while still others were black from beatings. For identification I was required to attach to the big toe of the right foot a label with the inmate's number; then, sometimes without help, I carried the bodies into the attic over the infirmary. The odor was indescribable. Twice a week a truck hauled these bodies to the crematory at Buchenwald. The attic was rather cold, but very quickly the corpses became green, bluish purple, blackish; some of them had enormous sores that continued to ooze onto the other bodies. Decomposition progressed rapidly. Before the body could return to dust, it had to rot.

One evening, having forgotten to attach a label, I was obliged to grope through the darkness to find in the pile of corpses one right foot that had not been tagged. I did not find it until I had felt all those rigid and cold bodies. After tagging the toe, I hurried to regain the company of the living.

Georges was very kind to me. Unlike most who had some function in the administration of the camp, he was considerate. Satisfied with my work, he prolonged my convalescence; this extension allowed me to remain in the infirmary for two more weeks. When he received a package from home, he shared it with me. It is hard to imagine how important the smallest diet supplement became. I was truly thankful that I had met Georges in the concentration camp. He not only befriended and encouraged me, but he also helped me to regain my faith in mankind. This gift of faith was more precious than were the packages.

While for me the days were passing in the comparative shelter of the infirmary, outside the snow did not stop falling. Every evening our comrades returned exhausted, quickly swallowed their much-too-small piece of bread, and threw themselves like beasts onto their bunks to try to regain a little strength or to forget. But, while it was still dark, the command to get up, "Aufstehen, los, los," jolted them out of bed into the cold. Dawn had not yet dispelled the darkness when they set out in worn-out shoes and ragged clothes to endure another twelve hours of cold and hard work. The same routine was followed every day, even Sunday. The prisoners could not know when, where, or how it would all end.

Albert succeeded in being assigned to block 2, where his bed was next to mine. At first he maintained his strength, but he was working a night shift in the quarry, and soon I could see that he was weakening. His health worried me. As an infirmary attendant, I often received a little extra soup, and most days I was able to pass it on to him. Despite his declining health, his morale remained stable and serene. Our friendship deepened through the daily battle of this somber season.

As an attendant, I learned how the infirmary functioned. It was, of course, supervised by a German kapo, assisted by Czechs, Poles, and a French doctor, our dear Dr. Cliquet, the only bona fide physician. But, because Cliquet was French, he had no authority, and he was restricted to bandaging. As for the others, whatever they knew about medicine and surgery they had learned in the camps! On the basis of his camp schooling, the kapo assumed all responsibility for diagnosis and even tried what seemed to me abracadabra experiments on the bodies that fell into his hands. Admittedly, the section of the infirmary reserved for him was neat, clean, and fairly well equipped, with instruments in place, but this orderliness was only a façade. In reality, it was very difficult to obtain health care, and the few medicines were reserved for the kapo's cronies. Sores, unattended month after month, often became infected for want of bandaging. How many young men died when an aspirin would have controlled the raging fever, or charcoal tablets would have checked the dysentery? In appearance, all that was necessary to provide health care was available; in reality, anyone who became ill could rely only on himself.

One day, I happened into the operating room, and I was able to observe how an appendectomy was performed. The patient was a

Russian. I saw the kapo approach, make an incision with his scalpel, rummage around with his forceps, and then withdraw for a cigarette break. While the attendants talked boisterously around the table, a Pole took his turn at manipulating several instruments in the abdomen of the young Russian, as if the operation were a way of killing time. The patient lay on the table for three hours, his abdomen open, and yet the "surgeons" never succeeded in finding his appendix. It was an incredible scene! Fortunately, he had been anesthetized, but many operations were performed without anesthesia. Who cares about the pain of others? Finally, the Russian showed no signs of life. The infirmary secretary would merely cross out his number.

I believe that the staff later attempted a similar operation that was no more successful. It was then decided that no treatment was available for appendicitis. Indeed, by contrast to the bungled surgery, the intravenous injections that resulted in the immediate death of the terminally ill at Buchenwald had seemed more humane. But euthanasia raised serious questions, for it has been employed to purge undesirables.

Our infirmary kapo was a would-be surgeon with fondness for amputations. Our lives depended on practitioners like him. Their criminal insensitivity made them valuable tools for the extermination work of the SS.

But the constant association with the dying was not a happy one, and the staff needed some diversions. The principal pastime of our infirmary attendants (I consistently exclude Georges and Cliquet) was to brew a drink of alcohol and honey—procured through theft or barter from SS provisions—and to become intoxicated. When the attendants were drinking, it was pointless to seek medical attention. The SS indulged the infirmary attendants, some of whom were avowed criminals. Although all of them were prisoners like us, they enjoyed many privileges while we were granted none.

Like most of the Germans in the camp, the attendants practiced homosexuality and satisfied their desires with the young Ukrainians, who generally acted like lords of the infirmary and often stole food from the patients. Assigned to distribute the soup, these scoundrels organized a bartering system for the food. The patients, deprived of their rations, were helpless. And when by chance a patient received a package, these unscrupulous favorites of the infirmary attendants demanded a portion of the contents and often confiscated the rest to share with their protectors. Thus in the infirmary, in the blocks, at the work sites, a privileged caste of degenerate Slavs flourished under the protection of their patrons. This caste caused the rest of us much hardship. To my knowledge, few Frenchmen accepted the ignoble role of homosexual servant, in spite of the advantages it assured—food and better work assignments.

The Russians, the majority nationality group, set the tone. With a few happy exceptions, it was their behavior that necessitated the unrelenting struggle for survival. For example, when an inmate died, those around him hastened, often before he had drawn his last breath, to confiscate all that he possessed. Not only were his pockets emptied, but his shoes and other clothing were taken. True, we were desperate, and he would have no further need of his possessions, but robbing the dying was inhuman.

This infirmary where no one was cared for was, nevertheless, the prisoner's best hope for at least temporary deliverance from work and inclement weather. But it was not easy to gain admission. Most of our comrades were acknowledged to be ill only a few hours before death, when there was no longer hope. Since there were no beds for the dying, they were laid in the infirmary corridor. The hall was always filled with people whose death rattles were borne on the icy drafts. They shivered and died in the midst of general indifference. There was no helping hand. There was not even a compassionate look given to these men, who had mothers, wives, and children somewhere!

Since my leg was healing satisfactorily, Georges said that he could not again extend my stay in the convalescent ward. Consequently, on December 20, 1943, I was ordered to return to work. Naturally, I was reluctant to abandon a relatively privileged position, but I was pleased to learn that Georges had chosen Albert to replace me. I was the one who had introduced Albert to Georges just when Albert had exhausted his physical resources and had become despondent. He would remain in the infirmary, first as an attendant, then as a patient, until the end of May 1944 when he would leave Laura. Henceforth, he would never grasp the handle of the shovel or the pickax. How could he have survived the quarry much longer? He owed his life to Georges at that time.

My return to the quarry was an ordeal, for I had lost my conditioning, and I had forgotten how long a day in the cold quarry could be. Unfortunately, I was assigned to one of the most demanding commandos, the *Walbrecht Grube,* which worked twelve-hour day shifts one week and twelve-hour night shifts the next. We performed the heaviest and most dangerous work in the shafts. This commando was truly pitiful, made up of unfortunates who had not succeeded in having themselves assigned elsewhere. These were the *Muselmänner,* as the Germans called them, not because they were followers of the prophet, but because they were human ruins at the end of their resources; dragging about in their rags and misery, they were already broken in spirit. One of the practices of the System was to assign the most difficult tasks to the weak, to the sick, and to those who were most defenseless. Some commandos, because of the work and the guards, were more demanding than were other labor details. In these cursed commandos in which an assignment of only a few weeks transformed the prisoner into a *Muselmann,* one died earlier than he would have died elsewhere. As it became necessary to replace workers even more frequently, each day those who were released from convalescence or the infirmary were without fail assigned to the *Walbrecht Grube* or to the Dany Commando. These commandos were invariably supervised by the most malicious kapos and foremen. Their penchant for sadism often indicated by the green triangle, these criminals took pleasure in inflicting suffering.

Thus the technique for exterminating human beings by forced labor was perfected.

All day long, poor, starving devils had to carry rails, push carts, and carry stones. When they fell because of the strain or because of illness, the kapo flailed them with a rubber truncheon. Many, attacked by dysentery, suffered pangs of torment. Each day the fatigue increased, the effort became more painful, the hunger was more piercing. Each day strength diminished and a relentless wave of despair eroded our morale.

The excavations in this mine were extensive. We realized that we were digging the foundations for an underground factory that would be sheltered from bombardment, but we had no idea what the factory's use would be. We burrowed many corridors and rooms; the site was a giant molehill in which one could become lost and from which there was no exit! The dimensions, the working conditions, the impatience not only of our kapos but also of the civilian supervisors—all of this gave us the impression that we were engaged in some diabolic enterprise deep within the bowels of the earth. It was an eerie spectacle, this scene of dark and tortuous chambers cut deep into the earth, corridors through which heavily burdened inmates gutted their way past numerous obstacles, passages in which the workers fell into pits that echoed the unrelenting hatred and the harsh bellowing of the kapos. In one corner, on the slimy earth, a man died; at the same time, a tilt-truck farther on crushed the foot of another. Next to him, a foreman vented his wrath on a poor youth whose strength was spent. Everywhere were the same suffering, the same hatred, the same pain. Powerful searchlights, creating fantastic images, illuminated the corridors into which the shafts led. The spectacle was dominated by the deafening noise of the pickaxes, the grating of wheels on the rails, and the shouts of the kapos.

The hours were interminably long, and it seemed that the end of the day would never come. Although most of the commandos re-

turned to camp at 4:00 P.M., when it became dark, we never returned until 7:00 P.M. Outside, the temperature was minus ten degrees Celsius; penetrating winds whistled through the shafts. After
three days in this commando, I knew that I could not long endure.
And my leg was bothering me again.

I decided to go to the secretary of work statistics, a good Czech. I
told him to which commando I was assigned, and I showed him the
open sore on my leg. The next day he assigned me to another commando. The transfer was another lifesaver! But, of course, it was
necessary that someone else be assigned to the *Walbrecht Grube*—
someone just released from convalescence, no doubt. Therefore, I
lived only because someone replaced me. But what other choice did
I have if I did not wish to relinquish the struggle for life? Indeed, we
did not want to surrender; we did not accept the inevitability of
death. We wanted to live, though certainly not at any price, for we
cherished some principles more than life itself. And because we re-
frained from some of the common practices—theft, coercion, in-
forming—we were sometimes at a disadvantage. But we resisted by
rejecting the System, which pitted us as enemies one against the
other.

Meanwhile, Christmas was upon us. It raised a flood of memories
and dreams associated with the tenderness of our childhood. Although until that time we had not been given a single rest day, on
Christmas we were granted a free half-day and a somewhat thicker
soup. Some comrades had recently received their first packages and
gathered together for the small, special treat that reminded them of
home. Like many others, I had to be satisfied with my bread ration
and my twenty-five grams of margarine. How strange it was to celebrate Christmas in this land of forced labor! Suffering, misery, and
death surrounded us; far away, many centuries ago, in a little Pal-
estinian village, was enacted the marvelous story of the birth of a
child who was Christ the Lord. But was it not precisely because men
were suffering, miserable, and held captive that God sent His son
to heal them and to set them free, "to bring out the prisoners from

the prison, and them that sit in darkness out of the prison house" (Is. 42 : 7)? Albert and I, seated on our straw mattresses, tried to recite from memory the Christmas story: "You shall find the babe wrapped in swaddling clothes and lying in a manger"; "Peace on earth, good will toward men." As some strains of the Christmas carols came back to us, we felt ourselves to be in communion with the universal Church, assembled throughout the world to worship her Lord. Thus, on December 25, 1943, Christmas came to us as a gift of glad tidings, of strength and peace.

My new commando was called *Walbrecht I.* The work was less strenuous and the workday shorter. Unfortunately, we worked outdoors in all kinds of weather. We were the unskilled laborers for a building project, and our assignment was to unload bricks, sand, and cement from the trucks. The detail permitted no idleness; we slung bags of cement weighing fifty kilos across the nape of our necks and we were obliged to unload the sand within a limited time. Furthermore, winter brought its own hardships. I recall that January 1, 1944, was an especially taxing day. When everywhere in the world people were enjoying the warmth of family reunions, we had to rise before dawn, gulp down a quart of tasteless liquid, and, after roll call, grope through a blizzard to the construction site. All day we unloaded bricks, which we threw from man to man without moving from our places. The temperature plunged to minus twenty degrees Celsius. Literally blinded by the snow, we worked like robots, no longer having any feeling in either our feet or our hands. In the evening we returned, exhausted and broken by fatigue. January 1, 1944, fine omen for the coming year! Our hearts drifted to the lost hearth; we were frightfully homesick for the family atmosphere and for the affection of our loved ones. What would this year of 1944 bring us? We believed that our liberation was imminent. In my prayers, I begged for freedom and for the strength to endure until the moment of liberation.

I changed commandos again, this time for the *Transport Maschinen Kolonne* to which I remained attached for five months. This brigade, rather demanding at first, became less taxing as spring passed, and in summer, when the commando was reduced to a few maintenance units, it became almost a rest station. What especially pleased me was that I was no longer required to use pick or shovel. We transported machines from the railroad station to their destination in the mine. We used jacks, levers, and pulleys, and we were supervised by civilians. Sometimes the work was strenuous, and sometimes it was less demanding; it varied. Still, I began to show the effects of malnutrition. I had no more strength, but the civilians who were in charge of us paid no heed. Indeed, they were generally abusive and brutal toward us; it was not only the SS who mistreated us!

But we suffered most from the cold! The winter was severe. Laura, situated at nine hundred meters above sea level, was exposed to all winds and inclemencies. Our clothing consisted of a shirt, undershorts, a pullover, trousers, a cap, and a jacket of lightweight, unlined striped cloth. The feet and ears of some of the comrades were frostbitten, and their hands were cracked. Our footwear, galoshes with wooden soles and canvas legs, was shabby. Our feet were in water almost all day. Naturally, there was no provision for socks or gloves. Therefore, we were obliged to make our own socks and gloves from rags retrieved from wherever we could find them—from the camp, from pieces of blanket, or from the quarry. Since the socks and gloves had to be mended every evening, we were always on the lookout for even the shortest piece of thread or wire. Only thus could one survive. Bathing, like keeping ourselves clothed, was an ordeal. We stood in line for a little water from a single outside pump; however, washing was essential to our morale.

Upon return to the camp in the evening, I met Albert. In his new assignment, protected from the elements, he regained his strength. Then, in February, he fell seriously ill. The frequent attacks of fever strained his heart. Georges and Dr. Cliquet provided the best care that they could give him, and his condition improved slowly. I went to the infirmary to see him almost every evening. At last he had the pleasure of receiving letters from home and his first packages. But since he had no appetite, he gave me much of the food, which was a great boon in this time of hardship.

On January 6, 1944, special stationery was distributed, and we were given permission to write ten lines in German. My letter, which finally reached my aunts, was the first news they had received concerning me since the previous August when the letters from Compiègne had reached them. Their answer to my lines of January reached me at the end of February. I cannot express how I was torn by reading and rereading their words, by rediscovering, in the land of exile, the existence of quite a different world where life was continuing, where cherished loved ones still held me in their affections.

Another important event was the arrival of my first package on March 11, 1944. With great joy I opened the box, packaged with love and imagination to supplement our insufficient diet. The contents of this beautiful package nourished my body and gladdened my heart. I felt strong and happy. Suddenly, because I sensed the love of family, I forgot the cold and the pain. The packages restored my vitality. I continued to receive them fairly regularly until July, and during these four rather mild months, my physical strength revived. But during the mild weather, it was essential to gain strength in order to survive the coming winter.

In block 2, I now lodged in a room of twenty-one inmates, of whom nineteen were French or Belgian; thus we were at ease with one another. This lodging was not at all like our previous dormitories. For several months, after a harassing day at the work site we enjoyed there a life of comradeship that I remember fondly. I must say that our circumstances were significantly ameliorated by the block leader, Lorentz, the father of several children, a German Communist, and a railroad mechanic, imprisoned for the last nine years. Of all the Germans whom I met in prison, he was one of the very few for whom I developed a high regard. Very often when we returned from work in the evening, Lorentz would have waiting a bucket of hot bath water, so that it would not be necessary for us to stand in line for a little cold water. He sought only to help us, and we loved him as if he were our father. We furnished our room with a table and some shelves made from the boards and the nails we were able to "acquire" (a euphemism in vogue) from the quarry and to smuggle into the camp. A stove was at our disposal, and when we were able to procure fuel, we could not only warm ourselves, but also cook. Most of us were now receiving packages, and those who received them shared with those who did not receive any. We shared a common table. Because we were Frenchmen who understood one another and who wanted to help one another, an esprit de corps developed. From time to time now there were Sundays when we were not required to report to the quarry. Schmidt was always careful to find a job for us. But, in the evening, more relaxed, we found ourselves in our room, and, thanks to the packages, we could gather round a hot drink and some crackers to sing the old songs of our homeland. When I thought of the hell the criminal kapos had made of block 1 and of block 3, which had become disciplinary blocks, I could appreciate our privilege. In blocks 1 and 3 at all hours of the day and night there were roll calls, screams, blows, and theft. The atmosphere in those dormitories was turbulent. In our block there were never screams or blows, and only seldom was there a theft. Because we were able to establish a society of Frenchmen, room 7 of block 2 was temporarily an island of peace in this forced labor camp.

One Sunday morning we were notified that a film would be shown in the evening. The SS had become attentive! At 5:00 P.M. there was a roll call to muster the one hundred inmates who would view the film to be shown in a building near the SS barracks. Having reported promptly enough, I was included among the privileged. But the dialogue was in German, the film was old, and the story was uninteresting; consequently, very few movie-lovers went to see the films shown thereafter. The SS would not accept our boycott of their cultural program, and a tragicomedy was now and again enacted as the SS and the kapos chased prisoners across the grounds to draft them for the movie detail. Since two hours of free time was rarely granted, most of us would have preferred to rest or to mend our tattered clothing.

At the construction site the same harassing life, the cold, and the misery persisted. One commando, the Dany Water Supply, specialized in extermination. A few days in that commando were enough "to send you up the chimney," as we said. This commando was in charge of excavating for the waterlines that would supply the underground factory. The workers were marched to a work site several kilometers from the camp. They worked with their feet in the snow all day long. Always standing, they ate their soup outside in the cold. Since their work site was in the open, especially alert SS guards and kapos with dogs were assigned to the detail. Schmidt systematically sent the weak and infirm to this commando. In March 1944, it was not unusual for this commando to bring back in the evening as many as fifteen dead. A comrade told me that the work area was marked by a trail of blood in the snow—blood drawn by dog bites. It was obvious at roll call that our ranks were diminishing rapidly. When would the mortality rate be checked? About one thousand men were currently in the camp. Transports arrived regularly from Buchenwald to fill the gaps caused by death in our ranks. It could be estimated that seven hundred or eight hundred inmates died between December and March.

Finally, Easter arrived, and for this holiday we were granted two days of rest—two days of splendid reprieve saluted by the sun. Nature gradually awakened from her long torpor, the snow melted, the earth warmed, and already the buds swelled with new sap. We were still to endure some unexpected periods of cold weather; the last snow fell on May 23. But already the advance of spring was prevailing; the specter of death receded with winter. Like convalescents, after much suffering we saw the light at the end of the tunnel. Despite all odds, life reaffirmed itself!

Easter! This year no bells summoned us to church, but mysteriously it was the great book of nature that, like a parable, confirmed the message. With several Catholic friends, we shared our hope and our faith in the resurrection. We believed that God had performed great deeds for us. And in this world, the same world in which the Son of Man had been put to death, "God made Lord and Christ Him whom we had crucified."

The beginning of spring coincided with the end of the reign of terror at Laura. The work was less demanding because the major tasks of building the factory, tasks performed under inhuman working conditions, had been completed. Our diet improved a little as potatoes replaced rutabagas in the soup. Henceforth, we no longer worked on Sunday, and we immediately felt the benefits of this reprieve. Furthermore, the mortality rate sharply declined. At this time, I was receiving one or two packages a week. In short, after all that we had been through, life now seemed almost bearable. We were full of hope, based on the conviction that we would not spend another winter in exile.

Unfortunately, Albert's health caused us anxiety. His heart faltered, and many times he hung between life and death. Dr. Cliquet rendered every service that he could perform for Albert; secretly, of course, the doctor administered shots and digitalis. Every evening I visited Albert in the infirmary and took him some dainties from my packages. He received packages also, but he had no appetite, and almost every time that he received a package, he asked me to give his ration of bread to some prisoner about whom he had been thinking during the day—sometimes a Frenchman, but other times a Russian or a Yugoslav who he knew had a special need. Despite his weakness, his serenity was remarkable, and everybody, regardless of nationality, loved Albert. What he did and what he showed himself capable of doing in the hell of the concentration camp reflected pure charity. Yes, I have observed that there is a love stronger than hatred, and indeed I learned this secret, which had been revealed to Albert, my best friend. I knew, furthermore, that if God should grant him the grace to survive, he intended to consecrate his life to God's service. But, at the height of his suffering, his soul attained such purity that God judged him ready for another service. On May

26, 1944, a convoy of the seriously ill was formed, reputedly destined for a rest camp. I was not to see Albert again. He died two months later at Bergen-Belsen. The farewell had been deeply painful for both of us. From the time of our arrest at the Spanish border, we had seldom been apart, and like two brothers we had shared all our plans. I wept, I believe for the first time in the concentration camp. Before leaving, knowing that every change meant confiscation of all personal possessions, he had entrusted all of his valuables to me: the letters from his mother, some linen he had received, and a Bible that had arrived in a package from Geneva.

I developed shingles, which became infected and caused such acute suffering that one day, when the burning had become intolerable and when Allied bombs were falling, I wished that the camp would be hit and that the bombs would put an end to my suffering. Finally, once again, I was admitted to the infirmary, and I spent twelve days there. It was there on June 6, at noon, that the kapo, greatly excited, told us of the Allied landing. Immediately, the news provoked a lively discussion, and each one explained his personal military strategy and made plans for his liberation. The first news transmitted by the German radio seemed encouraging to us, and the landing seemed to have succeeded. We were in a state of euphoria. Almost well, I left the infirmary.

We received two out of three packages that we were told to expect, and we greatly appreciated them. Letters from my relatives and friends were no less welcome. André Espaze announced the approaching birth of a child and at the same time requested me to be the godfather. His request gave me great pleasure, for it transported me to a land where people were still uniting to love and to give life. This land was in another universe but one that truly existed.

With great sadness I learned of the death of Emma, killed in an American bombardment of Nîmes; she left her husband and two young children. She was a very close cousin, and I received a package from her more than a month after her death. How many losses this war has caused!

We especially appreciated our Sunday rest. This respite was due not to a new SS concern for our health but to the fact that the factory did not operate on that day. Thus there was a pause in the dull and stultifying weekly routine. Now we were actually allowed to lounge all day, and fatigue duties were rarely assigned. We used the time to wash and to mend our clothes as efficiently as possible, and to cook whatever was in our packages. Since Albert was no longer with us, I shared with René Rio, a fine, cheerful young man, who received very little mail; we were quite compatible.

We often spent Sunday afternoon on the lawn in the sun. What an unbelievable change had taken place during the last few weeks. I had time to read the Bible that Albert had left with me, I could find silence, and I could meditate. We liked to talk with one another, and a spiritual communion developed with some Catholics. Among them my best friends, who were also from room 7, were Jean-Paul Garin from Lyon and Georges Nimals, a Belgian from Toulouse—both students of medicine. The atmosphere of the concentration camp does not foster friendship; therefore, there is nothing more precious than those friendships that develop despite the hostile environment. On Sunday evenings we gathered around the stove in our room, and we enjoyed singing the old provincial airs. While we tried to harmonize, our innermost dreams invariably projected us back to the land of our youth, to the land of our pride.

Again I was transferred from one commando to another, and our new work site was three kilometers away, near the village of Lehesten. We were opening a roadway across open fields, and we were not sorry to leave the bleak scenery of the slate quarry for a while. The work was not exhausting, and the supervisors were fairly reasonable. We especially enjoyed our contact with nature as spring was bursting forth. Even the SS and the kapos possessed some human impulses; more than once, as we passed a woods, they gave us permission to gather huckleberries or a few mushrooms—if we would not wander too far, of course! These were really the best days of my captivity in Germany, but these relatively good days were numbered.

Camp discipline was relaxed after an important change of personnel. For military reasons, we suspected, some officers of the Wehrmacht replaced some of the SS officers. Thus we noticed without regret the departure of Schmidt. The camp was orderly; we enjoyed the fresh air and the sunshine. We showered twice a week, and every Sunday clean linen was distributed to us. The diet improved significantly. Furthermore, a canteen was set up, where beer, onions, and sometimes canned fish were available. Paper money, valid only in the camp, was issued. Each week we received about two marks, which was not much, but along with the money gained through the sale of tobacco, the allotment enabled us to purchase a little extra food. Finally, we had some books and a little leisure. Under these conditions, we could survive.

By Herculean labor the underground factory had been completed. It was used for the final assembly and testing of the V-2 rockets. For this reason, the factory was under heavy military guard, and the workers were selected under safeguards that would prevent the leaking of the secret. In the compression rooms liquid oxygen was produced. The firing of the rockets occurred in two silos, which, in the shape of bunkers, rose at right angles, dominating the vast circuit of the quarry. The three-meter-high rockets resembled huge champagne corks. Thrust and performance were tested by the combustion of a mixture of alcohol and liquid oxygen contained in the tanks of the rockets. Each day, twenty-five or thirty tests were made. Before each test, the siren sounded the alert and everyone sought shelter. The effect of the ignition was tremendous; from the bunkers a fifty-meter stream of flaming smoke swirled downward, causing the stones to fly about in an infernal whirlwind. The power of these weapons terrified us, and the propaganda of Goebbels relied upon the frightening effect of these new weapons. But many tests, sometimes more than half of them, were unsuccessful, either because of faulty intake, defective mixing, or explosion at ignition, all of which frustrated the engineers, one may well imagine! Actually, despite the risks, there was much sabotage at

various stages of the production. In the machines that were allo-
cated to us, there was always a weak part, a screw not securely in
place, a misplaced bolt; no one ever knew who was responsible for
these errors. Furthermore, the quality of material left much to be
desired. In addition, there was the involuntary sabotage due to the
scarcity of skilled workers. Men not fit for combat were recruited
for the war industries, and we saw well-meaning peasants use glue
on joints that required solder. When the glued joints were subjected
to the thrust of the V-2, they ruptured.

The news about military developments gave us hope. In spite of
the rumors that filled the air, we gained some reliable information.
An Alsatian comrade worked in a shop where the SS radios were
repaired. Sometimes he could pick up London. This period was that
of the breakthrough in Normandy, the campaign in Brittany, and
the thrust across the Loire toward Paris. We were overjoyed!

The alerts multiplied by day and by night. Many times we could
see the flying fortresses in close formation and hear the distant
thundering from hammered cities. We sensed that the Reich's industry already had been dealt a telling blow. We were able to elicit from
civilians bits of information about the military situation. One of
them told me one day, "We know that this war is lost, but we are
already preparing for the next one." How much more were the citizens of the Reich willing to suffer?

We heard the names, one after another, of the liberated cities.
Then Romania surrendered. Her capitulation was such a shock to
the SS that blind faith turned to disillusionment. The atmosphere
had been tense since the July 20 attempt on Hitler's life, an event
about which we knew only through rumor. Now the SS sought revenge against a prisoner from Luxembourg who had showed joy at
the news of the capitulation of Romania. Naturally, the German
prisoners wearing the green triangles joined with the SS in retalia-
tion. All day this poor fellow, a professor in a Catholic college, had
to work under the verdict of revenge. He was beaten by the SS,
beaten by the "green kapos," and bitten by the dogs. When he re-

turned at evening, totally exhausted, he exclaimed, "They are going to kill me!" What could we say that would not sound hollow? The next day, the same torment was repeated. We were told that, after he fell from exhaustion, a German guard stepped on his neck to suffocate him, stuffed his mouth with dirt, and pierced his eyes with a bayonet. Finally, another guard put an end to him with a bullet. We who had hoped that we had witnessed the last of such barbaric acts were horrified and disgusted. An unsettling fear hovered over the camp. Everyone expected the worst and harbored somber premonitions. We had rejoiced too soon. The liberation, which we had thought to be at hand, now seemed very perilous. What was in store for us at the last moment?

In this setting, one of the most painful stories in which I was ever implicated unfolded.

For some time, the thefts of packages at night from under our mattresses had multiplied. During the day, no one left anything lying about; we carried in our knapsacks the little that we possessed. Since we were all French and all knew one another, it was difficult to suspect anyone. The thefts disquieted us because packages had arrived less frequently since the invasion, and once again we began to be hungry. One night, a comrade returning from the latrine surprised a young Russian in the act of rummaging around the foot of our beds. Our roommate immediately called out, and everyone jumped out of bed. We all knew him, a veritable scamp. He succeeded in escaping through the window. The German prisoner on patrol, who was alerted by the commotion, searched for the thief and brought him to us two hours later after we had already gone to sleep again. Several times the guard said to us, "Kill him; that's the law in German concentration camps." Meanwhile, we found under his mattress several cans of food and even letters recognized by their recipients. The camp guard, who had found the thief hiding in the infirmary attic, also discovered a supply of stolen packages there. The evidence was convincing. We were unanimous in our decision not to put the thief to death, but we intended to give him a lesson that he would never forget. We pounded his buttocks soundly before we released him and told him to stay out of our sight. We thought the matter concluded. Certainly, it was not frivolously that we took justice into our own hands. But could we have acted otherwise? Could we, without reacting, have allowed him to steal indefinitely? Our fate depended on these few grams of nourishment. Was it not our right to defend ourselves? In the morning we left for work. But during the day, Pierrot and I, who worked together, were uneasy. There was too much electricity in the air; events in France were developing quickly. We sensed that the SS guards were nervous.

Returning in the evening—tired from the day's work, the march, and the heat—we saw that four Frenchmen from another commando were carrying the Luxembourg prisoner, who had been killed that very day. Evil omen! Then we noticed that one of our comrades, a robust man, was being led half dead from the work site. We knew that someone had vented his anger on this man. We understood what was in store for us.

When the camp senior, the famous thief Ali, learned about the punitive action of the previous night, he responded in rage because he did not like Frenchmen and because he wanted to provoke a zealous reaction from the SS. Most of all Ali wanted to avenge the Russian, his protégé; that is to say, Ali used the Russian to indulge the most ignoble passions. He also took his share from the packages that he encouraged his favorite to steal. Thus, in his diabolical mind, Ali conceived of a plan to falsify his report to the SS. While we were at our work site, he searched our sacks and our mattresses and collected all the articles we had accumulated; knives, saw blades, an ax for chopping wood, a hammer, etc. He reported to the camp chief that we had fomented action not only against the Russians but also against the SS guards themselves. On the basis of this report, the SS chief ordered that each of us should receive ten lashes of the *Schlag*, that we should be assigned fatigue duty until night, that we should spend the night in a confinement cell, and that there we should wait for whatever might follow. The SS junior officer whom we called "the Italian" took matters into his own hands and promised Ali that justice would be swift. Eight of us from the same room were considered ringleaders. Our buddies, pale and frightened, gave us the news when we returned from work. The bell rang for roll call. We had just enough time to agree together that we would not utter a cry during the beating.

When all the prisoners had been counted, our eight numbers were called, and we broke rank to stand at attention before the camp commandant. There was total silence. What would happen? The commandant asked us if we had beaten the Russian. When we responded affirmatively, he cursed us and called us American mobsters. I was sent to fetch the whipping block. I ran to get it, and since I was nearest to it, I placed myself in position. Bent over the whipping block, my feet dangling, my skin was tightly stretched over my buttocks. One of my comrades was chosen to administer the ten lashes with the *Schlag*. "Hit hard," I told him; "otherwise, you too will be lashed." He tried, but against his will. He was as white as a sheet, and the punishment hurt him as much as it hurt me. Each lash bruised my flesh. Sharp pain flashed through my body, and I counted to three . . . four . . . five . . . ; no, this punishment was too much. Nevertheless, it was imperative that I should not cry out, for I was obligated to my comrades. Seven . . . eight . . . nine. I shriveled in anticipation of the blow yet to come, and I gritted my teeth . . . ; finally, it fell. But the Italian thought that since I had not cried out, the blows had not been heavy enough. He rolled up his sleeves and grasped the *Schlag*. He dealt blows that would have felled an ox. He had perfected a special technique of striking not perpendicularly but at a tangent, as if he were flaying a hide. I was crushed and dazed by the fury of his attack, but I was proud that I had not cried out. I thought that my companions would indeed be very courageous if the beating drew no cry from them. I knew what their silence would cost them. In turn they assumed their position on the whipping block, and not one of them allowed a cry to escape. The whole camp comprehended their courage. Certainly we had often witnessed floggings, but usually, after the third or fourth lash, the poor victim squealed like a stuck pig; usually, after the fifteenth or twentieth blow, he fainted. I was proud of my companions, proud that we had shown no weakness. But if I were required to endure the same treatment again, I would not dare to promise that I would not cry out.

Our punishment was not yet at an end. After roll call, which was prolonged so that everyone could witness this demonstration of justice, the SS guards took charge of the eight of us. They forced us to carry, at double time, tree trunks from a pile at the camp entrance to the building that served as a sawmill, a distance of about one hundred and fifty meters. On the second trip, although my strength was drained, I was expected to pick up an enormous piece of wood that I could not lift. My comrades were already running with their burdens. The SS officer lashed me with his whip. Still I could not lift the wood; it was too heavy. Finally, heaving desperately, I raised the colossal trunk and staggered toward the sawmill. The SS officer beat me all the way. Ah, one day the roles should be reversed, so that he might comprehend the misery! I swayed, paused, stopped, and started again. Passing before the line of my comrades, I noticed that all eyes were fixed anxiously on me as I resolutely struggled under my crushing burden to arrive, fully spent, at my destination. The SS ordered us to saw all the wood before evening, and they locked us in the shed. From time to time, they came to see how the work was progressing.

Pursued by the unrelenting hatred of the SS and of certain Russians whom Ali had incited against us, we despaired. At the end of roll call, a band of Russians clamored at our door, which fortunately was locked. Indeed, we were convinced that had they succeeded in forcing the door, we would have been dragged out and lynched. After what had happened to the prisoner from Luxembourg . . . ! But we decided to defend ourselves to the end. Broken by fatigue, with fear gnawing at my entrails, I was sinking rapidly into a bottomless pit of despair. To die would have been nothing if I could have been tenderly cradled or if I could have laid down my life for love. But to die under screams of fury, to be disowned, trodden into the mire like vermin, to be rejected by my fellow man . . . such a fate was more than physical anguish; it was an infernal death. And, nevertheless, such was my Master's fate when the waves of hatred broke over Him and bore Him to the cross and when the people whom He loved, His own people, cried, "Take Him away! Take Him away! Crucify Him!" Through His experience, I understood that I was not alone in bearing the burden of the human condition, that nothing could happen to me contrary to the mysterious will of God, Who accompanies us and Who is the Lord of history and of all mankind. God extended His grace to relieve me of the oppression that was overwhelming me. While we were sawing wood, I was able to witness to my comrades about this grace. One of them, a Catholic, added his words to mine. Inner peace came to us, and human hope was born again. Night had long since fallen when the camp police came to escort us back to our block. Everyone, including the Russians, had retired. Two or three later tried to taunt us, but otherwise the incident seemed closed. Our attitude at roll call obviously had made an impression. It was evident that the report against us had been fabricated. Nevertheless, by the law of the jungle, we had surely been sentenced to death; and it was, to say the least, unusual that the affair ended without further incident. Our roommates saved our soup for us, and they could not think of enough ways to express their concern. Before we went to bed, we compared our hindquarters. I bore the most scars, which for more than a month would be changing through all the colors of the rainbow. I could not sit for several days, and I could lie only on my stomach.

This incident occurred on August 26, 1944. On this day, Paris triumphantly acclaimed on the Champs-Elysées the tanks of Leclerc.

The tricolor waved again over our capital. When we heard the news, we found the strength to smile. We were avenged. Paris, the heart of France, had expelled the Nazis.

The next day was Sunday. Remaining on guard in our room, we used our free time to relax. The commotion seemed to have subsided. However, on Monday, an SS guard struck me several times and caused me a very troublesome day.

We were called to the office, where a report of the incident was to be filed in the presence of the loathsome Ali. The secretary, a Czech who knew us well, did not permit himself to be intimidated by Ali. Courageously, the secretary drafted a report in our favor. When the SS chief became familiar with the report, he said, "The facts were not presented to me in this light." Of course, but the damage had been done! It seems that later, the Russian in question, having continued to steal, was strapped outdoors, where, naked and without food, he was left to die.

We had suffered too much from this painful incident, we were too fearful that Ali would seize upon another opportunity to avenge himself, and the atmosphere of the camp had become oppressive when we were informed that a transport for another camp would be formed in two days. We welcomed the opportunity to leave Laura, where we had spent a few rare days that we called the "good times" only because they were somewhat less unbearable than the almost uninterrupted "bad times." We arranged to be part of the convoy. I distributed most of my possessions because all of our belongings would probably be taken away at the entrance of the new camp. The rumor spread that we would be in an excellent commando. Our only regret was that we had to leave behind some good comrades.

Mackenrode, Forced Labor Camp

I do not know where God is in this war because one cannot penetrate the riddle of the universe, but I do know that I can be struck only when He wills, as He wills, and where He wills.

—Alain Fournier, a conversation with Pierre Maury

We departed from Laura in cattle cars. The floors were covered with straw. In comparison with former transports, this one was relatively comfortable. We were given bread, margarine, and cigarettes; then the train pulled out.

Naturally, we were still under guard, but through the open door we could see the countryside. The Thuringian forest was indeed alluring, especially at this season. The journey lasted two days. We passed the immense Merseburg nitrogen plant, which must have covered several acres. The factory had been almost destroyed in recent air raids. However, we were happy to observe the destruction. We passed through the station at Nordhausen, and without delay our cars were shuttled to the camp of Dora, five kilometers from Nordhausen.

Thus we were in the notorious camp where many of our countrymen had died during the winter of 1943–44. Most of the French brought here—one group numbered from 14,000 and later a group numbered from 20,000—had been exterminated within a few months. At first Dora had been only an extension of Buchenwald, but it had quickly become as important as the parent camp. Dora, a veritable city, must have housed about 20,000 prisoners when we were there. We saw the camouflaged entrance to the tunnel where many human beings had experienced untold suffering. An expansive industrial plant had been scooped out under the mountain.

79

Later, when the camp was liberated, the Americans seized all operations before the Germans had time to destroy evidence. The Americans, who discovered about a thousand V-2's stocked in the plant, were astounded at the vast unsuspected underground corridors. The new weapons promised by Hitler and Goebbels—arms that would have sown terror to reap the impossible miracle—had been manufactured secretly in chains of subterranean factories across the entire Reich. Dora was an important link in this chain. I often heard from comrades transferred to our commando that this tunnel was a hell hole; the work required was the same type of labor demanded of us at Laura, but excavation at Dora had been much more extensive.

From the caverns there emerged daily the prisoner-drawn carts, bearing to the crematory their cargo of flesh, usually one hundred to two hundred bodies. In the hell that was Dora, the SS brutalized and exterminated.

After we had stood in formation for a long time, we were led to the camp office. What would happen to us? Would we be kept at Dora? The prospect hardly pleased us, but, because the winter was far off, life here promised to be tolerable. We were required to fill out a long questionnaire; then we were led to the shower and the clothing center. The shower was the entrance rite to the camp. Of itself, the shower was an excellent beginning, for the opportunities for prisoners to bathe were not frequent despite the grand affirmations of German hygiene! But the shower was a sort of baptismal rite by which the prisoner renounced the old man and put on the new man of the camp. The prisoner left absolutely everything at the entrance of the shower room, and at the exit he received new clothing. Farewell knapsack and such treasures as it contained! In anticipation of another winter, I had collected not an insignificant number of articles of clothing received from home or given to me by Albert: shirts, pullovers, undershorts, socks, gloves, and a balaclava helmet, etc. The Germans at Dora no doubt kept whatever they wanted and sold the rest. For the approaching winter, I would have only a shirt and the striped pajamas of those conscripted for forced labor. It may be fashionable to disavow material blessings, but life in the concentration camp depended on a pullover.

We were led to the quarantine block, where we spent the night. The next morning at roll call, we were informed that we would be leaving for another commando. I do not know by what incredible chance I recognized André Guyonnaud among the numberless ranks in the assembly yard. At the risk of being intercepted by the kapos, he succeeded in falling out of formation and in joining me. In a few moments, although he was in danger of being detected, he told me what had happened to him and informed me that Pastor Heuzé, who had experienced grave hardships, was now a block secretary because he spoke German. This rapid conversation filled me with joy and encouraged me. There were some of our brothers who were surviving; we were sustained by thinking of one another.

Then we were given the signal to march off. We had remained at Dora only long enough to have all of our possessions confiscated. Our column left the camp on foot, but—oh, how marvelous!—we were escorted not by the SS but by soldiers of the Luftwaffe. Once we had traversed the suburbs of an industrial city, we followed a secondary road bordered by apple trees. We stared wistfully at the inaccessible fruit, and from time to time we were able to pick up some worm-eaten apples the wind had blown onto the road. The rotten apples dulled our hunger and quenched our thirst. We were treated decently by the soldiers. The kilometers lengthened and followed one after the other, the sun was hot, our worn-out shoes caused our feet to hurt, and some prisoners had to walk barefoot. Furthermore, four of us had to carry a French comrade who was writhing with stomach pains. Late in the afternoon, we arrived at the village of Mackenrode. Without stopping, we had marched twenty-five kilometers. In the middle of a field, we came upon a barrack surrounded by barbed wire and four watchtowers. This very small camp made a favorable impression, even though we had been told that we were being sent to a factory.

At the entrance, we were received by an SS officer who ordered us to close ranks. We were counted and then counted again to ensure that all two hundred were indeed present. Ah! These interminable counts. Then we were divided into three sections. I was in the group that would remain at Mackenrode. The other two groups would report to the camp at Nüxel and Osterhagen, several kilometers away, both of which were engaged in the same enterprise. Once again, I was separated from cherished friends.

The camp was located just outside the village of Mackenrode. We could see the houses of the village, dominated by the belfry of the Lutheran church. During the following days I often contemplated the enigma of this steeple. It was not mine to judge, and I did not know those who assembled in the church, but how could the steeple, presiding over grave injustices, point the way to heaven!

We saw people working in the fields. These farmers intrigued us because for many months we had been cut off from the land of the living. This camp, which had been in existence only for a month, accommodated three hundred prisoners, of whom quite a few were French. One block had been built, and another was under construction. The farm land provided a suitable building site until tramping the ground drenched by the autumn rains turned the meadow into an impassable swamp.

Since the parent camps boasted all the attributes of permanent installations, this camp, by contrast, seemed temporary. A well provided drinking water in very limited quantity. We splashed ourselves and washed our soup tins in a still pond. By instinct, the French gravitated to one corner of the block. Because space was limited, two people shared each bed. My bedfellow, from Lille, had body odor and sometimes wet the bed. Oh, the minor inconveniences of communal life!

After roll call the next day, the commandos were formed. Predictably, the most unpleasant tasks were reserved for the new arrivals. One kapo insisted that he needed strong men. Since I was swollen with edema and therefore looked deceivingly robust, he assigned me to commando one, the most difficult, which worked in the forest. We marched three kilometers to reach a beautiful beech forest in which huge trees had been felled. A scowling foreman gave brief instructions while the kapo ostentatiously toyed with his club. Then we were ordered to trim all the branches off the trees and to stack the wood in orderly piles. But this assignment was only the beginning. Next we were to move the many enormous trunks that were lying on the ground. While we were wondering with what cranes or by what method of rolling logs we could move them, the kapo, foaming at the mouth, lunged toward us. He was enraged that we had not understood that we were to carry them. As one comrade attempted to protest that we could not carry out the order, a kick from the authoritarian boot instructed him that orders were to be obeyed. Such action, like the brute language, expressed the mentality of the prison staff. We had forgotten that here, too, and everywhere in Germany, we were only slaves, and we were expected to follow only one directive: "Shut up and suffer."

Under a hail of punches and kicks, we learned the technology by which ancient slaves constructed grandiose works. We slid studs under the trunk, and two of us on each side of the trunk grasped each stud. We placed the studs as closely as our ranks would permit. Fifty or sixty men could hoist the tree and carry it to the designated location. What an effort! This task demanded tremendous muscular exertion. The tall inmates, of whom I was one, were at a disadvantage. They bore the brunt of the burden for the short inmates and for those who only pretended to exert themselves. No sooner had we put down the first trunk than we had to hoist the second. There was no time to catch our breath or to talk about a better procedure. Indeed, the kapo found that there were too many of us for a single trunk and that the work did not progress quickly enough; therefore, he divided us into two teams. At first, we had carried the trees that were at hand or that were the smallest. Thus, at last, when we were drained of our strength, the heaviest trunks were still to be moved. In the afternoon, we were ordered to lift trunks that had fallen on marshy ground. Slipping and panting all the while, we risked dropping the trunk and breaking the legs of all the men on one side of it. The superman task was all the more difficult to perform because we were weakened by months of malnutrition. Our foreman was an irresponsible gypsy type, an impostor who seemed to find a sadistic pleasure in making us suffer.

Once again we had to ascend Calvary as the grimmest days overshadowed us. Surely, such duress would not last forever, but, in the meantime, we had to survive. My back ached, my arm and leg muscles knotted, and I was dizzy. My comrades were also spent. And always, "Los, los, schneller," with no letup! Indeed, we exercised our will until our will was broken. But every day had an evening. At the close of the workday, each of us lugged back to the camp a chunk for the kitchen fire. We literally dragged ourselves to the compound.

This routine was followed every day. Some Frenchmen who had been in this commando for a month were completely exhausted. The rest of us, like them, would not be able to endure. Many regretted ever having left Laura. For me, it seemed that there was nothing to regret. To remain at Laura had promised nothing. Now, without looking back, we should courageously accept our fate.

We were laying the roadbed for a new railway. We were urged on because the approaching winter freezes might hamper or interrupt our work. It seemed that this railroad was of some military significance.

There was one pleasant surprise—an improved diet. The soup served here was thick, similar to a ragout of potatoes with pieces of meat. Almost every day each of us received one and one-half liters of this soup. Three of us shared a two-kilo round of bread, but on Sundays, a loaf of the same size was divided between two of us. In addition, we received fifty grams of margarine and a link of sausage or a piece of cheese. Unfortunately, these rations were not to be continued, but even these portions were inadequate for young men who worked hard twelve hours a day. Some necessary foods, such as sugar, fats, fresh vegetables, and fruits, were not included in our diet.

I made up my mind to leave commando 1. When my shoe rubbed a blister on my foot, I made a huge dressing, and the whole day I exaggerated my handicap and my pain. The displeased kapo tried to force me to maintain the pace of the other workers, but I stubbornly continued to limp. The next day, to be rid of me, he transferred me to another commando. He did not want any *Muselmänner* in his commando, and I had accomplished my purpose.

Commando 6, to which I was assigned, also worked in the forest and performed the same kind of labor as that of commando 1, but under less brutal conditions. The work climate depended on the kapo. It was most disconcerting that we were supervised by fellow prisoners who demanded output only to gain the favor of our wardens.

I remained in this commando for several weeks. The work was tolerable despite all the disadvantages. Beatings were rare. In September we were still enjoying beautiful weather, and we appreciated this stand of magnificent beech. However, as the days passed, both our hope and our impatience increased. "The summer is ended, and we are not saved" (Jer. 8:20). Was the end of the war at hand? We had no reliable source of information, and the reports which circulated were often constructed from bits and pieces. But the camp environment caused us to lend a willing ear to the "latrine bulletins." We could not live without news; thus necessity was the mother of invention!

We thought that the Germans had been driven out of France and Belgium and that the front was no doubt along the Rhine. We wondered when the river would be crossed. I timidly suggested that the Germans would be able to make a stand at the Siegfried Line, which would offer them their last hope. But I was criticized as a pessimist, and my arguments were refuted by the bold strategies of my comrades. However, everybody agreed that we would be home for Christmas. This prediction inspired one of our number to describe the meal which would appropriately mark our return: "A turkey, well browned, stuffed with chestnuts and bacon bits . . . , with a good Bordeaux."—"Well, no, a Beaujolais, dear friend, it must be a Beaujolais . . ." Once this conversation began, it seemed never to end.

Air raid alerts became more frequent. Not a day passed that we did not see above us Allied aircraft in close formation, like a shimmering tide streaming across the heavens. We were proud to hear the powerful, rhythmic drone as it rumbled from horizon to horizon and left in its wake an impression of tranquil power. The sight and sound of the Allied formations comforted us despite the thousand vexations of our daily round. The planes also inspired us to dream of escape: "Ah, if only they would drop a line that we could climb!" For a long time after the bombers had passed, we could see glistening in the sky thousands of bands of tinfoil intended to intercept the radar. The tinfoil floated down, wheeling and turning. "Ah, if only they would drop sandwiches!"

What made the Germans furious was that never did a single Luftwaffe plane appear during an alert. After the all clear, two or three fighters would cautiously parade. Three or four times we witnessed aerial combat, a strange, celestial ballet, danced to the rhythm of machine gun bursts or to the swelling rolls of strafing planes. Crash, explosion! The formation flew away, leaving behind a heap of smoldering metal. "Americans kaputt, Americans kaputt," our guards exclaimed, but each time a black cross burned across the earth. In our hearts, we savored the joy of these little revenges. We knew that the day of great revenge was approaching—the day of victory, the day of liberation from contempt.

The French had a reputation for being loquacious, and we were. We welcomed every opportunity to gather for discussion. The topics of our conversation were most diverse, and each one spoke freely of his native country and his profession. Here, where social conventions were of no significance, we expressed ourselves without inhibition. Therefore, my understanding of people increased as I learned about life-styles of which previously I had known little. I was in immediate contact with journalists, officers, merchants, politicians, unskilled laborers, farmers, and even pimps and international smugglers.

Sometimes, when labor conditions permitted conversation, we had lively discussions even at the work site. A twenty-seven-year-old fighter pilot from Lyon told us one day how he had shot down nine enemy planes during the "phony war"; as a result, he had received the Legion of Honor at ceremonies in Nancy and had been promoted to lieutenant. While stationed in London, he was promoted to major by de Gaulle. Later, he was shot down and went into hiding but was apprehended and deported to Germany. Several others spoke of their activities in guerrilla warfare, in parachute drops, in sabotage, and in the Resistance. These accounts bolstered our faith in the final victory of those who conspired to achieve liberty.

One way or the other, the work proceeded. A new commando, number 16, was formed, and I was assigned to it. Each morning we had to walk eight kilometers to our job, and, of course, each evening, eight kilometers back to the camp. Our worn-out shoes alone would have made this march painful, but our exhaustion made it torturous. The roadbed for this section of the future railroad ran across open fields. Each one of us was assigned a definite work quota. Each day, working as a team of two, we were required to load a certain number of tip trucks with twenty-five to thirty cubic meters of earth. This demand was unreasonable, for the ground was so hard and stony that first we had to break it with a pick. We were digging our own graves in the German earth! I could still swing my pick fairly well, but many of my friends were noticeably weakening. What would happen to them if we should be forced to spend another winter here? We were so famished that once again our hunger became an obsession. It was absolutely essential to relax our pace, but we were watched too closely. Strange as it may seem, some worked rapidly just to make trouble for others. At Laura, as well as here, I had observed that some prisoners—poor intimidated fellows, robots of the System—killed themselves with work when they could have limited their output. We marked them well, for by increasing production norms, they involuntarily became our enemies. They worked to their own detriment, and most of them did not last long.

Since we were fortunate enough to work under a reasonable foreman, I did not try to transfer to another commando. Admittedly, in spite of ourselves, our team worked decidedly harder than the others, but thereby we gained some small advantages. The SS supervisor distributed tobacco to us as often as an unprecedented three times a week. I did not smoke, but tobacco was a valuable currency; with two or three cigarettes, I could buy a liter of soup. Perhaps it is surprising that soup was for sale in the camp. However, there was nothing we could do about the black market; we were governed by the law of our environment. The German prisoners, who distributed the soup, set aside several containers for a company of profiteers, the Slavic dishwashers, who ate what they wanted and blackmarketed the rest.

In the fields that surrounded our work area, the farmers finished digging potatoes, and from time to time we discovered some that were left. What a windfall! Our foreman, a decent fellow, asked the guard's permission to roast the potatoes in the embers of a wood fire while we continued to work. Thus for several days we enjoyed a significant nutritional supplement, though no more than we needed to carry on the work. The potatoes helped us to maintain our health, while our comrades in other commandos began to look sickly.

Not all of our guards were from the SS; some, Luftwaffe reservists, annoyed that they had been reactivated, were not zealous in their duties. Although beatings were rare, we still distrusted the malicious kapos.

The road to the work site wended through several villages. The few inhabitants who appeared along our route showed nothing but scorn for us. One day a little girl approached to spit on us. But from time to time we met some French prisoners of war, who tried to encourage us: "Not much longer, boys! They're retreating." Sometimes, when the guard of a small commando dozed, the prisoners of war defied the segregation order. They came over to talk to us and even slipped us some bread. Ah, it was easy to recognize our fellow Frenchmen! They were all alike, with the beret cocked on the side of the head, their carefree walk, their hands in their pockets, their open and direct gaze. In the debacle that was destroying the soul of Germany, the French prisoners of war were not among the vanquished!

The camp organization still left much to be desired, and with the return of inclement weather, a life of sheer misery began again. In the morning, we mustered under a driving rain, marched off to work under the deluge, worked twelve hours outside in the downpour, and returned soaked to the bone. Our tattered clothes were drenched, but there was nothing into which we could change and not even the smallest fire by which we could dry ourselves. Fortunately, because there was one blanket for every two prisoners, I could partially undress for the night, but imagine how I felt when the whistle blew me out of bed before dawn and I was obliged to put on the same wet rags.

The camp became a marsh, and roll call in this clay into which we sank up to our calves was a dreaded ordeal. The mud invaded our barracks. In theory we were allowed to relax on Sunday afternoons, but in practice we were kept so busy that Sunday was often more exacting than were the workdays.

Massive clouds that presaged no good for us continued to gather. In November again our plight worsened. The first frosts followed the torrential rains. On November 10 a heavy snowfall brought disappointment as we realized that another winter was upon us in this inhospitable land. What would the season inflict on us? How many of us would see spring?

The thermometer dropped well below zero. As a harsh wind blew the last leaves off the trees, I recalled these lines from Lamartine:

> This is the season when all things fall
> Before the rising winter's blast;
> From the tomb sounds the wind's icy call,
> Reaping the living to the last.

Our clothes, torn to shreds by the forest work, had not been replaced. Not one change of clothing was to be found in the camp. For three months we had been wearing the same shirt; we had no pullover or rain gear. The frigid dampness of the snow flurries penetrated our bodies. The water was so cold that not even the heartiest dared to bathe. We were so infested with vermin that we scratched ourselves raw. Because my shoes had no soles, I was walking in snow and mud. Since my feet were in an ice bath all day, I suffered from a perpetual head cold. Fortunately, I had learned very well how to blow my nose without a handkerchief; of course, we had none, and every rag that I could find I used to wrap my poor feet. It was more important to protect the feet than to use a handkerchief!

We could not have understood these deprivations if we had not experienced them. Our struggle against the unrelenting elements knew no quarter. The five long months of winter, the one hundred and fifty days that we were determined to survive at all costs, loomed before us like a lofty ice wall to be scaled with naked hands. My only aspiration was to live until Easter. To some of my comrades this distant date seemed out of reach, but setting the goal helped me.

René Cler, a veterinarian who had come with me from Laura, was one of my best friends. The SS commandant had appointed him camp physician, a position rarely assigned to a Frenchman. Gracious and dedicated, he accomplished what could be done with his limited supplies. One day a Russian whose arm had been broken when he had been struck by a club was brought to René, who complained to the commandant that medical treatment was unable to heal wanton injuries. Result: the commandant issued an order that brutalities inflicted on working prisoners must cease. To have René at hand was very reassuring; he administered the best possible care.

It was increasingly difficult for me to walk; therefore, when the daily sixteen-kilometer trek became impossible, I arranged to transfer to another commando. The snow, which covered the ground, delayed work on the railbed. In addition, the small locomotives which towed our dump trucks often could not run because there was no coal. We sensed that deliveries in warring Germany were not dependable. Our masters contented themselves with overseeing the maintenance of finished track sections which rain and frost were damaging. Once again it was necessary to grade the eroded slopes and embankments. Our numb fingers pained as we grasped the tool handles; yet it was impossible to find the smallest piece of material with which to improvise gloves.

One day the roadbed, undermined by water, collapsed under a locomotive which overturned. The fire in the boiler spewed onto the fireman, a fine young Italian prisoner. He screamed. As his clothes were removed, his skin blistered and peeled off in scales more than three-eighths of an inch thick. His face was scalded; his appearance was frightful. He pleaded with us to ease his pain, but we could not even touch him. He craved something to drink. Poorly sheltered, he lay waiting for two hours until a truck arrived to transport him to the infirmary at Wieda. We rolled him onto a blanket, and the truck bore his piercing cries out of earshot. He died that evening.

We heard almost no military news. What was happening at home? We hoped that the general mobilization would accelerate the final victory. However, we talked about the future less at this time; the current realities were cold and hunger.

Fortunately, some Red Cross packages arrived when we least expected them. I received three, almost completely empty. Nevertheless, the effect on our morale was appreciable. We no longer felt forgotten in a corner of besieged Germany; invisible ties across the impassable borders bound us to our homeland.

Suddenly, a very painful boil appeared on my neck. At that time we were carrying crossties. For several days I could not raise my head, and my right shoulder seemed paralyzed. René diagnosed the ailment as a very serious anthrax, and he admitted me to the convalescent ward. I was too miserable to appreciate the rest. Furthermore, the straw mattresses on which we lay all day were infested with vermin. The lice invaded my bandage and then tracked the pus everywhere. René decided to send me to Wieda, the camp administration center, where the infirmary was located.

Thus on December 6, an icy day, I left Mackenrode for Wieda. Since I would not need clothing in the infirmary, I was forced to leave my vest and my trousers for another prisoner, and I was hoisted, half-naked, into the open produce truck. As the vehicle sped along, I crouched as well as I could against the cab. Upon arrival, I was so paralyzed from the cold that I had to be lifted down.

The small camp of Wieda, several kilometers from Mackenrode, accommodated about one hundred occupants: kitchen workers, infirmary aides, clothing warehouse managers, and administrators for the three other camps. After the ordeal of this trip—if I had had a fever, I would have died en route!—I realized the most delectable moment imaginable. I took off my clothing to have it disinfected, and I took a bath in a tub of hot water. Oh, the sweet sensation! Blood circulated through my numb members and I was alive again. To bathe with soap and water from head to toe was a luxury I had not enjoyed for several months. Only those who have suffered from filth can understand the ecstasy I felt. After I was given clean sheets, the doctor examined me. Fortunately, once again the physician was a Frenchman, Dr. René Autard, from Gap. After administering a local anesthesia, he used his scalpel; I grimaced. During the following days, he extracted deposits of pus until I was almost cured. He informed me that the anthrax had produced two channels as deep as the length of his index finger. I wondered that my vital organs had not been affected. After the treatment, I could move my shoulder and neck again. I was very fortunate at that time to fall into the hands of a French doctor.

In the infirmary I enjoyed great tranquillity. While outside the wind turbulently drove the snow, and my comrades, caught in the cogwheel of interminable, exhausting hours, struggled, I rested in the warmth of a real bed surrounded by other beds that were occupied by other persons who peacefully rested, who relaxed, and who did not cry out. In this strange, plush atmosphere, I rediscovered the essential elements of life: warmth, food, rest, and spiritual tranquillity.

I spent two weeks in bed. Even though the anthrax no longer required bed rest, the doctor permitted me to stay as long as there was a bed available. The attendant was also a Frenchman and was very dedicated. I should not have been treated as well if the personnel had been Polish, for example. I accepted with unending gratitude the favors granted me. I did not even think about the fact that these peaceful hours were passing too quickly; tomorrow would take care of itself. I let myself drift on a wave of sleep, for I needed to compensate for past deprivation of rest.

As patients, we often were given extra soup and sometimes even milk. Because of the proximity of the kitchens, we were better served than were the distant camps, although their need was as great as ours. Furthermore, the appetite of some of the patients was poor. Therefore, at Wieda, at that time, those who were hungry could eat as much as they wanted. Consequently, some days I ate four to six liters of soup and often two rations of bread. Admittedly this was not a varied diet, but, in the absence of other choices, it was substantial enough to cause me to gain weight. The food and rest caused me literally to puff up. When I was discharged, my face was so bloated that my friends, who hardly recognized me, asked if I had a toothache. Even a foreman one day assigned me an easier task because he thought that my teeth were abscessed. I was careful not to enlighten him! I was not as well as I appeared to be; the edema created an illusion. However, I possessed recuperative powers, and I was recovering from the effects of the terrible month of November.

News from German radio stations was broadcast through a loudspeaker into our room. To our astonishment, only the victorious campaigns of the Wehrmacht in Belgium were reported. As the occupation of no important city was ever announced, we concluded that we were listening to the propaganda of Goebbels, who had little of which to boast at this Advent season. Indeed, every day we heard the bomber formations, and often we heard the distant explosions. Surely, the Germans could no longer restrain this force which carried the war to the heart of their country and presaged its inevitable ruin.

One day, the radio transmitted a splendid organ rendition of a selection from Bach. By the magic of music, I was transported a thousand leagues, into the sparkling light of purest religious emotion. Once again I experienced hours of grace. I thirsted for the physical presence of the Church. Even more acutely, I thirsted for that Kingdom for which the Church yearns—that Kingdom in which the hymn of the Beatitudes will never be silenced.

> My soul thirsteth for God, for the living God: when shall I come and appear before God? My tears have been my meat day and night, while they continually say unto me, Where is thy God? When I remember these things, I pour out my soul in me: for I had gone with the multitude, I went with them to the house of God with the voice of joy and praise, with a multitude that kept holyday. (Ps. 42 : 2–4)

On December 23 I was discharged from the infirmary. I had confidence; I must wage the battle against winter for only one hundred days! With my restored strength, perhaps I would remain healthy for a month; afterward, it would be necessary to survive by force of habit.

While I was waiting to be sent back to a work camp, I was instructed to prepare vegetables for the kitchen—an easy assignment that lasted only two days. Many were willing to resort to any deceit to remain at Wieda rather than be sent to a commando. At Wieda I met Pastor Henri Orange of Lisieux. He had been discharged from the hospital at Dora, where he had been confined with tuberculosis.

He was a living evidence of what God does for His own. For more than a year, he had been subjected to the merciless routine of the concentration camp, where, even though he was a clergyman, he was spared nothing. Although he was afflicted by all sorts of ailments—he should have been on a diet, and he should have been excused from all work—he survived nevertheless!

While we were peeling a mountain of potatoes, we exchanged views, and I was impressed by the similarity of our experiences. When we met in the morning of December 25, he said to me, "The society in which we find ourselves is the reflection of hell. People who cannot tolerate one another are, nevertheless, forced to live together here. Hell is a world that has banished love, a world where there is no place for God. But He has come anyway. Christmas is the extravagance of love."

Thus, we spent our second Christmas in captivity, in an enemy land, in a world at war, behind electrified barbed wire, under the terror of the SS. Perhaps I needed this experience to comprehend how necessary Christmas is. This descent into the abyss of our human condition was also necessary. The paradox of this particular Christmas drew me to the cross.

On Christmas Eve, I received a small Red Cross package, which enabled me to celebrate the day with a modest dietary supplement. Another sign of grace!

We were required to work in the morning on December 25, but we were free in the afternoon. Suddenly, without warning, I was notified that I had ten minutes to prepare for departure. I was disappointed that I would not be able to spend Christmas Day undisturbed at Wieda. I had to face another change, another adaptation; I had to prepare to submit to the rigors of the miserable life in a commando.

Osterhagen, Disciplinary Camp

If God does not exist, what is the meaning of all this suffering? It is meaningless; oh, my God, it is meaningless.

—André Schwarz-Bart,
The Last of the Righteous

At high speed the truck was transporting us toward one of the three subsidiary camps (I did not know which one) administered by Wieda. Secretly I was hoping to return to Mackenrode, where cherished friends, especially Dr. René Cler, awaited me.

Christmas! The word rang in my heart and clung to the frost-bent fir branches. In the little villages through which we passed, we saw decorated Christmas trees in the windows and rosy-cheeked children who were sledding. A familiar whirring filled the air, and hundreds of bombers appeared, sparkling in the sunlight and trailing clouds of vapor. For more than an hour this majestic, formidable stream flowed. The English were delivering their wartime Christmas gift to the Germans. What an impoverished Christmas for mankind! The exploding bombs drowned out the angels' song, and Satan led the bacchanalia.

Suddenly, observation towers appeared across a deserted expanse. We dared not believe that we were approaching Osterhagen; we dared not pronounce the name that would have stuck in our throats. Osterhagen, the infamous correction camp, the disciplinary camp of sinister renown! Nevertheless, simply because it was necessary to replenish the ranks, because the monster had to be fed continuously, I was sent to the most hellish camp.

Sheltered from any curious observers, three barracks were secluded in a hollow, a veritable cavity of hell. Not a tree was in sight—nothing but an icy plain, a barren expanse. The scene was wretched. Here not even the Nazi flag was to be seen. The individual no longer had any worth, and no one even tried to deceive him. His was a living death.

Upon arrival, some prisoners came out to gaze at us. We were immediately struck by their filthy appearance. They were thin, their clothes in tatters, their eyes haggard. Of about thirty Frenchmen in the camp, I recognized some whom I had known at Laura. Right away, they inquired about the military situation. "It is hard here, very hard," they said. "We manage, but we can't hold out much longer!" With my full cheeks and clean clothes, I was very conspicuous. But I was not optimistic; in a few days I too would be dirty, ragged, tired, lousy. I was accustomed to the faces of prisoners, but here more than anywhere else their expression was that of hunted beasts. The inmates bore the marks of immeasurable suffering. What a Christmas gift—to be stranded at Osterhagen!

Nevertheless, even here it was the birthday of the Christ. The commandos were not working. Some of the prisoners were reminiscing about past Christmases and family reunions. How lonely we were, centuries away from celebrations filled with our childhood delights!

Some Catholics, including Father Amyot, invited me to celebrate Christmas with them. Seven or eight of us gathered—secretly, of course—in the shed used as a lavatory. One of us stood guard. The old religious superstitions had no place in the new order! Amyot recited the eternally wonderful story of the nativity; a comrade hummed "Minuit, chrétiens," and in prayer I laid before God our suffering, our rags, our filth, our fatigue, our exposure, our hunger, our misery. All that we had to offer the Christ Child was our denigration and despair, but we knew that it was because of such degradation that He had come into the world.

After I had swallowed my soup, I met the camp commandant. In one of the blocks, the German prisoners had trimmed a tree with paper flowers. These inmates, along with the guards, gathered around the tree to sing a few strains of carols. Deplorable hypocrisy! Truthfully, I suspected that the guards had had quite a few schnapps. Finally, the commandant stood and in a husky voice addressed us: "You are our enemies, but we force you to work with us toward the destruction of your country, toward your own destruction. We have only one leader, Adolf Hitler, who is providentially destined to save Europe." For almost half an hour, he elaborated on this theme. Not by a single word did he indicate that he understood our situation as prisoners. He spoke only of the urgencies of war, etc. At the end, he asked if we had fully understood him and if we were ready to obey. The Germans and some of the Poles and Ukrainians sang out "Ja." The French said nothing; we were thinking, nevertheless. The fact that we were prisoners bore witness that we had understood for a long time!

The next day I reported to my new work site. In effect, the work was an extension of the Mackenrode project. Construction was long delayed by the freeze; therefore, for a week we were kept busy with odds and ends. I was able to buy a tattered pullover from a Russian, and canvas mittens were distributed to us. New Year's Day provided another occasion for remaining in the camp. Such a relaxation of the work tempo was quite unusual at Osterhagen.

Instinctively the French gathered together in a corner. January 1, 1945, I said to my fellow prisoners, "Cheer up, comrades; today we greet the year of our liberation." I believed what I said, but some were skeptical. They were thinking only that they had heard that same prediction for 1944, and more than one thought that without exception we would remain in prison to suffer and to die. "You're just coming from Wieda," they retorted. "You'll see after you've been here six months." Alas! They were not far from the truth.

January 2, we learned that the work site was temporarily closed because the snow and ice prevented any work with the machines. There was a lively discussion about the possibility of our being sent to Berlin. That suggestion did not please us at all. Although we believed that we could not fare much worse there than at Osterhagen, we dreaded another camp transfer with all the unknowns, the plunderings, and the unpleasant work assignments. Fortunately, we were not relocated.

One morning we were marched to the train station, where we boarded a special train that conveyed us about twenty kilometers to Niedersachswerfen, where we worked for another firm. We passed through an industrial region in which we saw many work sites and camps. Everywhere were barbed wire, guard posts, and the standard barracks. Not only did we gain a view of Germany at war, but we also gained a vision of the promised land!

For six weeks we worked at the construction site between the camps of Dora and Ellrich. Ellrich had succeeded Dora as the extermination camp. In passing Ellrich, we noticed near the entrance a large fir tree trimmed with electric bulbs. We were told that two prisoners, accused of sabotage, were hanged there on Christmas!

Until mid-February, we were routed at 4:00 A.M., herded into windowless boxcars, forced to work all day in the cold, and corralled into the same crowded cars at night. Required to leave camp early to avoid missing the train, we waited long on the station platform in a bitter north wind. Our guards were without pity. Having responsibility for a troop of forced laborers in transport, they wanted at all costs to prevent escapes. These tiring trips were added to our fatigue, undernourishment, cold, work, and vermin.

For the first few days, I worked under an infamous green kapo, a criminal, tall, gaunt, cynical, impatient fellow with piercing eyes and jutting jaw. He was quick to strike. If we looked up for a second, paused, or spoke, he pounced on us, his arm raised to strike. What a plague! Only those who drove themselves to the point of collapse were left relatively unmolested. It was essential to conserve the strength to work consistently enough to avoid being noticed. Every evening, back at the block, the green kapo took out a notebook in which he had written the number of each prisoner who had not worked hard enough that day. Often the same numbers were recorded day after day. Many were those of Frenchmen, most of whom were ill and at the end of their strength. Each of these hapless inmates would then receive five to ten lashes of the *Schlag* and sometimes would be deprived of soup. There was no shorter route to the crematory.

After the hardship of the day, silent and helpless, we were forced to witness these acts that bruised the bodies of our comrades and broke our hearts. The green kapo, this tall rogue, wielded the whip with an impassive countenance. He demonstrated no feeling other than his dedication to duty.

Finally, I transferred to another commando only to fall prey to a perfect scoundrel who hated Frenchmen; but since he was less zealous, he did not harass us persistently.

We were unloading stone near the entrance of the Dora tunnel. Every morning, we saw the civilian night shift exit and the day shift enter. Among the conscripted employees were many Russians and Poles, but we guessed that there were also some Frenchmen. Sometimes in passing we overheard snatches of conversation. One worker, pointing us out to another, said, "Well, look at those poor souls!" Since the guard was not looking at me, I called, "We have been in prison for two years; almost all of our buddies are dead." "Don't give up, pal, they're retreating," he responded. Of course, we knew that they were retreating, but we wanted details, names of cities, the regions. We wanted to calculate when the Allies would arrive.

We quickly emptied the stone from the cars onto the railbed, but we were obliged to wait for each load. However, the supervisor forbade us either to build a fire with the wood scattered about the work site or to put our hands in our pockets. The icy wind took our breath and blew the snowflakes hither and yon. We were literally chilled to the bone; our bodies were as cold within as without. What words could express our daily suffering? Only by grim determination did we survive; our nervous tension produced a physical and moral insensitivity.

The horrors of the preceding winter began once again: tingling in the extremities, paralyzing cold, frostbitten feet, fingers, and ears. Each morning it was painful to put on our shoes. One young eighteen-year-old Frenchman could not refrain from crying out. In a commando at Riga he had suffered frostbite of the feet and one hand. Each evening, in order to promote circulation, I vigorously rubbed my tingling feet. I was amazed that I suffered frostbite only on one leg.

The wind blew through our ragged clothing as if we had been naked. To protect ourselves, we moved constantly, hopping on one foot and then the other, slapping ourselves on the shoulders, rubbing our arms, and running, but at the same time expending the least possible amount of energy. I was assigned to a small commando to break stone with a sledgehammer. Although the work was difficult, we were not unduly pressed. I had a dispute with the foreman, who complained that I did not know anything about the work. I told him that, since I had been a student, no one had ever taught me the stone-breaking trade. "Students are good only for burning," he responded without hesitation. He had well learned the lesson of his distinguished master, Goebbels: "When anyone mentions culture to me, I draw my revolver!"

As often as possible, we worked with our friends. While we were working, we exchanged impressions and ideas. The subject that proved inexhaustible, our favorite topic of conversation, was the art of cooking. After we debated the chances that the soup would be thick or that we would be given a sausage link instead of margarine, each discovered in himself culinary talents.

"What would you say now to chicken in wine sauce?"

"Ah! Talk to me instead about sausage and sauerkraut!"

"Well, before the war, for my sister's wedding, we served . . ."

". . . Next, you mince the onions and sauté them in grease over a low fire . . ."

"At our house we use only goose grease."

". . . Then you thicken the sauce. Don't forget a large box of Parisian mushrooms with diced ham. Last, I add a glass of Armagnac . . ."

"Will you please repeat the amounts?"

Thus some of us rattled off exotic recipes; the hungrier we were, the more ingredients we listed. And we made up recipes for soufflés with Grand Marnier or for kidneys in Madeira. I had never before heard of some of these concoctions! No doubt our recipes called for too much of our favorite ingredients.

We were so preoccupied with our hunger that only by making a deliberate effort could we talk about anything else. To avoid reality, we reminisced and we planned. Of course, the escape tactic used most often was to hum popular songs at the risk of being sharply called to order by the kapo. The memory of faded loves deepened our nostalgia. We also recited from beginning to end poems learned in school. This exercise was much more challenging to our memory. What joy we found in the recitation of these poems! We needed to confirm our inward liberty. Furthermore, we dreamed endlessly of our return. When we regained our freedom, we would travel, we would visit one another, we would do things together. How few of us would be able to carry out these plans!

Camp rations diminished daily at an alarming rate. Was the decrease deliberate, was it due to the approaching battle lines, or was it because of the season? After February 1 we never received more than three hundred grams of bread—not a large portion, at the most four or five slices of this heavy bread. The soup was little more than clear water with a few pieces of potatoes swimming in it. Never before had we suffered as acutely from hunger as we suffered during that period. Everybody, including the Germans, grew noticeably thinner. Ah! To eat! To eat!

Soon after I arrived at Osterhagen, I was put in charge of one of the two French tables. No doubt I was chosen because, just arriving from Wieda, I looked healthier than most of my comrades, and because I knew some German. It was my responsibility to distribute the food to about fifteen Frenchmen at our table. In the morning, I got up before the others and went to the kitchen for the bread and margarine. In the evening, I supervised the distribution of soup in the mess tins. The breaking of the bread was a veritable rite, carefully scrutinized by every eye. Generally, whoever distributed the bread served himself last, and sometimes we drew straws for the crumbs.

Our strength failed rapidly, and many lost courage; the mortality rate increased. Two more long months before the worst of the winter would be over, but could we persevere even two more weeks? Our faces were gaunt, our skin was like wax, our eyes sank into dark sockets. Dysentery once again afflicted us. Had we struggled and suffered and overcome obstacles only to die here?

Then unexpectedly I was again receiving an occasional small package from the Red Cross. Packages were usually half-empty when we received them, but the little that they contained was a veritable treasure. As I opened the packages, predators jealously lay in wait, hoping that I would drop some portion of the contents! I wanted to devour all of the food in some quiet corner, but I felt obliged to share. I distributed a portion to those friends who had the greatest need. Although the packages helped, a few spoonfuls of sugar or marmalade could not quiet a long, ravening hunger.

At this time, I chose as a close friend Amaro Castellvi, a Spaniard whom I had known at Laura and at Mackenrode. He was a perfect companion, who had suffered much since the Spanish Civil War. He had been forced to flee Spain, and he had been interned in France before he had been sent to German concentration camps. Because of previous misfortune, he was accustomed to hardship. I shared my packages with him, and in turn, he helped me to defend my precious possessions against those who day and night sought to steal from me. The Russians were expert thieves! Despite tremendous temptations, Amaro was perfectly honest with me. We supported each other morally and materially, and indeed I believe that our friendship helped him to survive an especially difficult period when he had reached his limits. Would that I could have helped others likewise!

Hygiene was so deplorable at Osterhagen that we were infested with lice—a veritable plague of huge, black-crossed lice that multiplied rapidly. They ran everywhere and nested in the smallest seams of our clothing. They devoured us, especially in the armpits and around the waist. We scratched until we bled. In the evening, after work, we picked them from our bodies and smashed them. In vain! If we killed a hundred, a thousand replaced them. We scooped them off by the handful. They laid eggs by the thousands in the stitches of my pullover. Day and night we were on fire. We scratched ourselves and became infected. We were hopeless. They were sucking our life from us; we were walking corpses. I feel sure that some comrades were literally devoured by lice.

Cold, hunger, lice! As if these were not enough, we still had to endure the chicanery of the German prisoners. One Sunday when we were not working at the work site and the guards by some chance had not assigned fatigue duties, the kapos called for clothing inspection. Their pretext was that our clothing was attracting the lice, and they used their inspection to take everything from us except the basic issue: that is, a shirt, undershorts, and a pullover. It was with great frustration that I relinquished a second pullover I had acquired, a thin one that provided little protection against the cold. Some comrades were robbed of shirts and pullovers sent from home. Their protests served only to invite blows. From the wool of our pullovers, the Germans had socks made for themselves by two or three Russians who had learned to knit or crochet. I was outraged against those who thus condemned us to die from the cold. Was it true that they did not know what they were doing, they who had to share our fate? But who could understand the conscience of these German criminal kapos—a conscience the passing of time, the environment, and the force of habit had distorted? Had not man come to terms with this godless universe much as the infirm grows accustomed to his helplessness and the neurotic to his neurosis?

For the intensely cold weather, the only clothing that I now owned was a shirt with torn sleeves, a worn-out, short-sleeved pullover, ragged undershorts, a jacket, trousers, and a hooded, unlined coat of the infamous lightweight striped material. Yet the temperatures frequently dropped to twenty degrees below zero. The worn-out shirt, which for several months had been inseparable from my body, was filthy. Some comrades had worn the same dirty shirt for six months, for at Osterhagen it was impossible to maintain the simplest hygiene. There was no water in the camp; the only liquid that gained admission was the infamous morning coffee. Sometimes I sacrificed a quart of this brew to dissolve some crusts of dirt. Furthermore, since January I had been afflicted with boils that plagued me long after my liberation. Boils covered my back. Five or six at a time would appear and would cause fever as they drew to a head. As I felt them with my hand, I found that they were as large as little eggs. I was miserable, but, of course, since there was no medical care at Osterhagen, I was obliged to work in spite of the intolerable pain. When, by contorting myself, I was able to squeeze them, I gained some relief, but I had nothing, not even a piece of cloth or a scrap of paper, with which to dress the sores. My back oozed, the pus saturated my shirt, and the lice tracked through the muck. I could not know how intensely Job suffered, seated upon a dunghill as he scratched with a potsherd his burning boils, but I knew that I had reached my limit of physical suffering.

How can I even attempt to describe what I have survived? Would the reader believe me if I confessed that more than once in preparing these memoirs for my family I was seized by despair and tempted to destroy these pages? Why should I continue to write? Why, moreover, should I write about one incident rather than another? Why should I record a particular detail or memory? Why should I put in terms of common usage what the normal mind refuses to imagine?

Crematoria, gas chambers, torture, medical experiments, sadism, hangings, heaps of flesh and bones, are the elements of the horror story of the Nazi concentration camps. Our sick appetite, which, unless tempered by compassion, craves the sensational, is whetted by the ingredients of such a diet. However, what was hardly sensational, what no outside reporter could have perceived, was the pitiful banality of our daily life: the morning whistle that jolted us out of bed after a restless night of cold and lice; a quart of tasteless brew with which to gulp down the daily bread ration; wet feet, bare heads for the endless roll calls in wind and hail; the pale dawn departure of those condemned to death; the tools, our supervisor's commands, the kapo's screams; the interminable, burdensome hours that weighed upon us like a ball and chain—hours that stood still—9:10, 9:15, 9:20. Days, weeks, months, seasons, and years spent in waiting! We were filing away at an interminable chain of time of which each link represented the consummation of human suffering. Finally, there were the paralyzing cold, the debilitating work, boils, lice, and the waves of physical exhaustion that swept over us. Day by day comrades paled, well-loved voices became silent, eyes closed forever. And if we escaped for a moment into daydreams, we were brutally brought back to the stark reality of hatred, of forced labor, and of pervasive corruption which entrapped us in this derelict universe. We were crushed by the weight of our human condition. We wanted to struggle free, but always we were obliged to begin again, like Sisyphus, who had to roll the rock to the top of the mountain only to find each morning without fail that the rock by its own weight had rolled back to the valley.

When, finally, after all the efforts, the pains, and the small victories, the end of the working day came, we had to muster our dead, the poor dead who could no longer regroup themselves, and we had to drag along our sick. Like frightened cattle, we stiffened our back against the blows. At still another roll call we stood at attention, bareheaded under the elements. Then there was the jostling for the liter of hot water, billed as soup, and finally the stampede into the dormitory to claim a bed. Osterhagen, unlike better-organized large camps, was governed by the law of the jungle. Only the strong or those protected by the strong could sleep on a straw mattress, for the mattresses were in short supply. The blankets had long since been torn into pieces for foot covering. The Germans hoarded the few blankets that had been salvaged. Although the unheated barrack was frigid and our thin bodies provided no padding, Amaro and I often slept without a mattress on the hard floor. As we pressed against each other, one coat over our feet and another across our shoulders, we were grateful if the cold did not deny us a few hours of oblivion.

One day on the railroad near Dora, we saw a convoy evacuating prisoners from a camp in the East. In open cars covered with snow, some phantom forms still moved on a pile of rigid bodies and skeletal limbs. We were filled with silent distress. Someone said that the evacuated camp was called Auschwitz.

As of February 15 we no longer went to work by train. We began once again to work at the Osterhagen site. A period of great duress was brought to a close, but the end was not yet. Fortunately, on February 20, the barracks as well as our clothing were disinfected. We took courage.

However, the work demanded of us was excessive; we had to make up for lost time. Most of the prisoners were extremely emaciated and weak. Hunger plagued us now more than ever before. We grabbed our bread and devoured it. In all eyes lurked a predatory gleam. One Frenchman, arriving with a convoy from Breslau, which had been evacuated as the Red Army approached, told us that in his camp the hunger had been so unbearable that he had seen some prisoners feed upon the charred remains of those killed by flame throwers. Another told us that some of the Russians assigned to clear the ashes out of the crematory searched for bone marrow. Each story was more shocking than the previous one. I did not witness these acts, and I thank God for not burdening me with more than I would have been able to bear, but I could believe the accounts.

We seized everything that appeared edible: grass, roots, rutabaga skins, potato peels. The first dandelion shoots were a delicacy. We would have eaten the stones if possible!

At that time three of us were especially close friends. For Beckett, as for Amaro, I felt a deep affection. Beckett, a young Frenchman from Doulens, was a Protestant of English descent. The three of us always worked side by side. We encouraged one another and helped one another as much as possible. Often, as we reported to the work site, I tried to recall a passage of Scripture, and I suggested a motto for the day. Together we were stronger to ward off despair. What a thirst for justice, for peace, for love we shared! What a thirst for God! Admittedly, we were not heroes of the faith. Our spiritual life, like our physical life, vacillated. We were destitute, brutalized by misery. All of our senses were dulled. Our memory failed so dramatically that sometimes I stumbled over the lines of the Lord's Prayer. Nevertheless, even though circumstances restrained us from expressing our faith, it was there—pure and simple, stripped of conventions, solid—a faith that through hours of anguish and doubt wavered but did not fail. On the contrary, our faith sustained us in dark moments when the world seemed to crumble about us. Faith is a mystery. Experience convinced me that my faith was given to me, that it did not come from me. Before we went to sleep Amaro and I always brought before our compassionate Lord not only our requests—we always had many!—but also our gratitude and our intercessions for our family and friends. Indeed, there was always reason to thank God for answering our prayers!

I asked for the strength to endure to see my family and my native land again. However, I had learned to say, "Thy will be done." Once or twice, discouraged by the obstacles, I resigned myself to die in captivity. After all, the goal had been achieved—France had been liberated from the Nazi plague. Nevertheless, before I died I wanted to write to my parents to apologize for any sorrow that I might have caused them and to tell them that I had kept the faith.

The end of winter at Osterhagen was a nightmare. On March 2 my commando had to unload carloads of gravel. We were facing a raging wind, and the temperature was very low. On that one day, six of our comrades, five of whom were Frenchmen died of exhaustion on the job. To the twenty remaining Frenchmen, the loss was great.

Once again the camp was populated by the living dead. Every hour in every nook and cranny somebody was dying, often unnoticed and without even the touch of a friend's hand. I tried to reassure Amaro by telling him that spring was at hand, but he did not expect to live to see it. What then, if he died too? But no, together we would endure by force of will until March 31, the date we had set as our survival goal. Easter would be April 1. The weather would moderate; life would become less unbearable. Only twenty days, nineteen, eighteen . . . we lived moment by moment. Each evening, at bedtime, I remarked to him to reassure myself, "One more day has passed and we're still alive." Surviving was an act of desperation. Successive small triumphs threaded the tapestry of our life. It was indeed true that "sufficient unto the day is the evil thereof." It was possible that tomorrow would be another hopeless, difficult day, that the kapos . . . that the supervisors . . . that the cold . . . Nevertheless, we could experience nothing worse than what had already passed.

At last, a sort of general apathy spread across the work site. In order to conserve what strength they had left, the prisoners exerted themselves as little as possible. They were now too weak to swing their pickaxes, and the kapos were too weak to shout their commands. Even the supervisors and the SS no longer tried to prod us. Their spirits sank as the German people experienced the greatest disillusionment of their history. Therefore, we did as little as possible. We kept an eye on our guards, and when they were watching us, we pretended to work. There was no other solution. Some days, I hauled only three or four cartloads of dirt. Unfortunately, some prisoners were so intimidated by the threat of physical assault that they continued to work themselves to death.

The commandant was merciless. Never admitting that anyone was ill, he required everyone to report for work. Every day, he condemned the sick to certain death.

How can the tension of those last days of March be described? In January, when we heard about the Russian advance into German territory and the threat to Berlin, our spirits rose. But then it seemed that the front became stationary. The threat to Berlin was real, however, despite the temporary halt to allow for the transport of material and provisions for a renewed offensive. We knew that nothing would stop the Russians once they resumed their march. But when? How long we waited! Indeed, we would not be able to survive more than a few days.

One air raid alert followed another. Frequently we heard the bombardments. Several military convoys traveled through by rail. One night a violent explosion shook our barrack. The next morning as we went to work, we saw a still-smoldering locomotive on the track. "They didn't miss that one!" People scurried hither and yon like ants from a ruined anthill. We even saw peasants in carts who were fleeing from the East, and we guessed that the Americans had attacked near Cologne. Our will to live until we should be liberated was strengthened, but how long would we have to wait? If only we could have known! I thought that there was cause for optimism now in spite of all the past disillusionments. However, I suspected that the end would not come before June.

Survival was an obsession. One evening a fellow prisoner would confide, "It's all over. I can't hang on any longer. I'm never going to see my wife or my parents again." He dared not add what he was thinking: "Neither will you." Resignation was condemnation; those who did not determine to live slipped away. Death came quickly to them. We tried to build up each other's morale: "Don't worry about tomorrow; just live for today. Just try to get through this ordeal. Someday all this will seem like a nightmare, a dark cloud that passed over, a bitter memory. Don't give up; be determined. You'll see France again, old pal!" We tried to conjure up the memories of happy days: a joyful family meal, a Sunday morning in a sunny little provincial village, walks in the springtime. We lost ourselves in recollections of literature, of painting, of sports, of all that was dear to us, the activities of our youth groups, the shining hours of spiritual communion. Sometimes the memories cheered us, and sometimes they made us homesick as we vacillated between hope and despair. However, hope triumphed, even though it was unwarranted and foolish. We were fanatically hopeful.

We sensed that a great event was about to take place, that we were at the birth throes of a new age. Although our plight still seemed hopeless, we believed in the promise. There was something apocalyptic in the denouement of this grand, cosmic drama. The beast of nihilism had been bridled, but it had not yet had its full of hatred and blood, and it wanted to convulse the world in its death throes. Those whom I could not call my comrades, the German prisoners, threatened to kill anyone who spoke a word against Germany. The kapos warned us, "We know that we will be hanged when the camps are liberated, but beforehand we will make you pay." Then one would brag about killing twenty prisoners a day while another would boast of killing thirty.

Still my friends were dying. March 25, Palm Sunday, it was Marcel Brossard's turn. Thirty-one years old, a board member of the Reformed Church at Angers, he was one of my few remaining friends. Now I would never again hear his pleasing voice or shake his hand. He had received a picture of his beautiful family, and he had proudly shown me his six children. The youngest, Françoise, had been born after Marcel's arrest. All of his thoughts had been directed toward his family, their future, and their faith. Dear friend, what would you not have given to caress their curly heads! His life flickered out like a spent candle. Like his uncle who was here in January and his cousin—his uncle's son, who was with us only a few days—Marcel was no more. I implored God: "Art Thou a just God? Why dost Thou conceal Thyself? How long wilt Thou permit Thine enemies to triumph?"

Every death should be noted separately. Each comrade died in lamentable conditions and in the midst of immeasurable suffering brought about by the implacable hatred of our executioners. The unmitigated anguish of my fellow prisoners compounded my own despair. How glorious will be the day of reckoning when God will wipe away all tears!

Sometimes, in the somber hours when there seemed to be nothing for which to live; when, after the battles waged with determination, even the will became inert; in the hours when discouragement, like a swelling tide, overwhelmed me and drew me into the abyss of human despair; when I was hurdled down a precipice of distress—in these indescribable hours, several times, suddenly, unexpectedly, there appeared an inward light that rescued me from the depth of human misery in which I was drowning. Ah, if only the skies would open and Christ would appear in His glory! An awesome vision, an unbearable sight, desired, yet dreaded, brighter than a thousand suns! If only Christ would return! His return, after all, would provide the only true victory, the only hope that sometimes, in our human impatience, we want fulfilled immediately, as if it were not enough to know that no power in the world can prevent the fulfillment of His promise. Lord, teach us patience. Teach us the obedience You learned from Your suffering!

At the end of March, the miracle for which we had prayed was unfolding: a few of us were still alive. Once again I received a package. Why were some of us more privileged than were others? Were we more deserving than those who had died?

The first few timid rays of the sun warmed our hearts. The few trees we were able to see from our work site swelled with rising sap. Under the melting snow, a hidden life was awakening. With great emotion, we perceived nature's plan to write a new page.

Finally, March 31 arrived—the target date that I had chosen five months earlier. What a long five months! Our ranks were thinned. Now, more than ever before, we must look to the future.

Sunday, April 1—Easter—we were given a holiday. Something

was in the air, a feeling that something new was about to happen. Our little band of Frenchmen regained confidence. We prepared to receive the resurrection that already stirred within us. Our Lord had passed from death unto life, and He had promised us a present as well as a future life. We were borne on wings of hope. It was good that some days were less stressful than the others.

The End of the Night

Liberty, I write thy name!
—Paul Eluard

On April 2 and 3, we resumed work as if nothing had happened, but a thousand signs pointed to growing unrest. The civilian guard (*Volkssturm*) of the village had been armed and had assumed posts along the main road. More and more refugees from the East passed. Their antiquated carts gave way to proud automobiles driven by refugees from the immediate neighborhood. One train followed the other, loaded with equipment from abandoned factories. Fifty meters from the camp, a single fighter plane strafed a locomotive. Several times a day, Allied aircraft appeared. At night we heard the thunder of nearby artillery. It was clear that the front was pushing closer. The whole country was in a state of alert.

On April 4 at roll call, the SS stayed in their quarters. We were told that we would not work. We trembled with joy, but I cautioned the French, who were quick to show their feelings. We could not be sure how the Germans would react.

Not to work was the most desired and necessary privilege, for the work was killing us. Wednesday, April 4, was a memorable day, the beginning of the end. The next day also we remained in the camp. Apparently, the commandant was awaiting orders. We nourished the secret hope that those orders would never arrive and that the Americans would liberate us, perhaps within a week, perhaps within three days.

We saw several infantry columns retreating down the road toward the west, in the direction of Kassel. Then we saw a few tanks. The air raids were now very close. When a call for volunteers to haul water was issued, I responded because I was curious to learn what was happening in the village. Motor vehicles of every description, packed with miscellaneous items, sped by in spectacular display.

The Wehrmacht was in disarray. As I observed the bedlam, my lips curled in an ironic smile because we also had experienced the flight of soldiers and civilians, a flight that had choked our highways. Now we were avenged. However, a soldier who noticed me frowned reprovingly, and I resumed an air of indifference, for I was still a conscripted laborer. It would be better to proceed inconspicuously. I searched the faces for an admission of defeat, for a sign of remorse, for some evidence that those passing were not mere robots. In vain! Robot obedience was the disconcerting characteristic of this doomed regime. This people had placed faith in the leader and his mystique, and by a visceral reaction they continued to believe in him because they needed to cling to something now that the boat was swamped and they were hopelessly drowning. This faith was totalitarian, and its collapse could make room only for nihilism.

As we were going to bed, the rumor ran through the camp that in the morning we would march to Wieda. Actually, the rumor proved true because the order had been given to evacuate the region. I succeeded in snatching a blanket, and with my soup tin and spoon—indispensable utensils not to be forgotten—I set out. With no reluctance, no backward glance, we happily took our leave of Osterhagen, where we had suffered intensely. We marched off into the unknown. What was our destination? What would happen to us during the following days? Would we indeed be liberated by the Anglo-American forces? Accustomed to obeying a fate over which we had no control, we thought little about the uncertainty of our future. Regardless of where our uncertain course would lead, we were determined to endure until the end of the night.

The first stretch of fifteen kilometers led to Wieda. There we met prisoners who had just arrived from two other camps. I found several friends, very emaciated, but the death toll in their camp seemed not as high as in ours. In the evening there were roll calls, and we were divided into groups for the next day's march. As the SS prepared to evacuate the camp, we loaded equipment on the trucks.

About a thousand prisoners were assembled at Wieda. The camp was too small to provide beds for everyone. When night fell, everybody wanted to find a place to sleep. All of us crowded into the so-called dormitory. Clusters of human beings clung to the beds, of necessity stacked one on top of the other. All of a sudden, in the middle of the night, we heard a prolonged splintering sound, and we were enveloped in a cloud of dust as if a bomb had fallen. The beds on one side of the room had collapsed under the weight of their tenants. Cries rang out. Beckett, groaning, his sides crushed, walked by us. In the morning, when we could see, we discovered that some prisoners had been crushed to death. Until one-half hour before the accident, Amaro and I had lain exactly where the accident happened. Since we could not sleep, we had changed our location. If we had remained at our first spot, our chances for survival would have been negligible. Had we moved by chance or because of some secret premonition? Why was my life spared several times by similar reprieves before I regained my freedom?

The next morning we set out again, strictly held in formation by the SS, who did not relax their vigilance. Amaro and I marched side by side. For the time being, the pace was not too rapid, and everyone could keep up. We had left the ill at Wieda; they were to be transported later in army trucks. We marched north along a secondary road through the Harz Mountains. We passed through beautiful little towns, such as Braunlage, with its pretty chalets, scenery to which we had become unaccustomed. Other groups of prisoners marched ahead of us. No doubt they were from Dora and Ellrich and had been evacuated in the same direction. Night fell; we halted on a meadow, where, under sharp surveillance, we reposed under a starry sky. The blanket was too small for both of us, and it was so chilly in the mountains that it was difficult for us to sleep. In the morning, we noticed that a skim of ice had formed on a nearby pond. Without anything to eat, we resumed the march. The dying were left behind. Fatigue weighed upon us. Our legs were like lead. It was only by a painful effort that we dragged ourselves forward.

Frequently, to avoid being sighted by Allied pilots, we were ordered to the shoulder of the road.

In the evening we arrived at a small factory where a Dora commando worked. There, among Poles and Russians, was one Frenchman. He was thrilled to be able to speak to his countrymen.

We spent the night there. However, before we slept, there was an uproar in the darkened factory. Although we were all famished, the German prisoners had confiscated the entire soup ration. The ensuing commotion caused the SS to intervene with shots, dogs, and shouts. Everyone sought cover. Once again, we went to sleep hungry.

The next day the sick arrived by train. They had killed a kapo in their boxcar. Furious, the German prisoners, who saw the hour of reckoning approaching, incited the SS against us. The atmosphere was tense. How would this scenario end? Some insisted that we were surrounded by the Americans; others were convinced that there was still a free corridor to Berlin and that we were headed there.

After another long march, we arrived on April 9 in the city of Wernigerode, where we were corralled into cattle cars. Compared to others that we had known, they were reasonably comfortable; at least there was room to be seated. In each car a junior officer and an SS man stood guard. For three days we rode the rails; we made long stops at stations, some of which had been completely destroyed by bombs. We were dying of hunger. For three days we had been given no bread and only a half liter of soup. The German prisoners, who had found some potatoes in one of the stations, cooked them on a stove they set up in our car. I exchanged my last hoarded cigarettes for the peels.

In plain view a pursuit plane downed a flying fortress, and we watched five parachutes float earthward. The SS on our train raced to capture one of the parachutists. A large redhead with a graceful gait, he passed within three meters of me. He was supremely indifferent to the blows of his captors. The SS escorted him to the front of the train, where they confiscated all that they could use of his possessions. I felt proud to have seen one of our liberators.

We passed through Magdeburg, with its still-smoldering ruins. What a wasteland of desolation and isolation was this site on which a great city had recently stood! Most of the walls and chimneys were still standing, but the roofs had collapsed, and through gaping holes we could see charred partitions. Now in their own country the Germans were beholding the face of war.

From Magdeburg, the convoy took the spur line which went through Gross-Ammansleben—Neuhaldensleben—Röxforde—Letzlingen.

We were still traveling north. Conditions in the boxcar became unbearable with the groans of the sick, the stench, the hunger, and the thirst. Conditioned by two years of concentration camps, we were like stupefied beasts. Several times the dead were hauled out and stacked by the dozens in the rear cars. And the nights—oh, those long nocturnal stops in open country, then the dull grinding of axles announcing that the ghostly convoy would resume the journey into the unknown! Only the dull hammering from some distant air raid roused us from time to time from our lethargy. The farther we advanced, the farther removed seemed the long-awaited day of reckoning. If only I could have known that Wednesday morning, April 11, 1945, what was in store! There was a rumor that tank spearheads had been seen to the north, and there was a false rumor that tank units had also arrived at Magdeburg, through which we had passed the previous evening. Since about noon, our train had stood on a siding at Letzlingen. Everyone was disheartened, depressed, and drowsy. To avoid becoming further depressed, we thought of nothing.

In the morning we heard the familiar roar of bombers and the sound of explosions. The detonations caused our boxcars to vibrate, but we did not suspect that the rail ahead of us had been destroyed.

It was perhaps five o'clock in the afternoon when a conversation between soldiers attracted my attention. Something beyond my wildest dreams was about to happen. The junior officer and the SS man who guarded our car took all their belongings—haversacks, soup tins, blankets—and, leaving us alone, went to the rear of the train. They were leaving us alone for a moment—amazing!

Since they did not return, I decided to pull myself up to the ventilation window on the other side of the car and to look out. What I saw will always remain seared in my memory: five or six SS were conferring, and one of them, right before my eyes, nervously tore the eagle and swastika off his sleeve. An SS officer removing the sacred insignia of his mystique and of his power! An SS repudiating his identity! Could I believe what I saw?

I was overwhelmed, dumbstruck! There was not a minute to lose. Through the slightly opened door I could see the countryside and some small thickets. I shook Amaro, and, before he realized what was happening, I was urging him on: "Grab a blanket and your soup tin, and let's run." He wanted to gather up the leftover potato skins, but there was no time for hesitation. We jumped onto the roadbed. Like us, prisoners from other boxcars were escaping—especially the Russians, who were most interested in breaking into the commissary car. Nobody paid any attention to us. I still could not comprehend what was happening. Some German prisoners had mixed wood alcohol and sugar with water in a pitcher! I filled my soup tin and then passed the pitcher to Amaro. The mixture quenched our thirst and revitalized us.

But freedom was yet to be won. We ran rapidly away from the train to the nearest thicket. We could not let this moment of opportunity be lost. We had not gone three hundred meters when familiar, guttural voices cried halt. Several sharp reports confirmed that someone was shooting at us from the rear. We had no choice, for we knew what awaited us if we returned. We ran as fast as our poor trembling legs could carry us. Fortunately, the undergrowth was thick, our guards had no dogs, and we were not the only ones seeking refuge in the brush. After a breathtaking run of at least twenty minutes, we could hear nothing, no sounds of pursuit; we stopped to catch our breath in the dense forest.

I was not subdued; on the contrary, the foolish audacity of our attempt went to my head. For several moments I was literally drunk from the regained freedom, and I expressed my delirium by throwing my arms about Amaro and by running from tree to tree to prove that I was not dreaming. The awaited moment, the desperately hoped-for day, had arrived. We were experiencing liberation. It was within our grasp. Suddenly, all the pain, suffering, and fatigue rolled away. The death odor dissipated. I solemnly proclaimed to the trees of that fraternal forest: "This day, Wednesday, April 11, 1945, at 5:00 P.M. we are free men. We have overcome!" Amaro, weaker than I, was less demonstrative, but his joy was great.

Later, I learned that although a few prisoners, like us, had fled to the woods, the SS, before seeking their own escape route in the face of the advancing Allies, had panicked and had massacred all those remaining in the convoy, many of whom were our friends. Among those killed was Beckett, a poor lad who during his captivity had endured many hardships: typhus and two serious accidents before the last one at Wieda. He had fought hard to survive; yet he was deprived of the final earthly consolation of seeing his family and his homeland again. Dear Beckett, your young, sad face haunts me. I remember you as a symbol of a sacrificed generation, which, created to flower in the beautiful sunshine of God, nevertheless knew only tears and suffering. I know your sad look, your youthful eyes that closed forever when you were only twenty years old. I learned then that there are trusts that I must keep.

The enthusiasm generated by our escape was short-lived. We were not yet really free. We were in a no man's land, or more likely, we were still in the province of the SS, who might regroup and hunt us down. We did not know where the Americans were, where the front was, if there were still fighting, if the war were over. Why had we felt such great joy only to lose it and to find ourselves as helpless as before?

"Where are we going?" Amaro asked. I answered, "Due west," and through the trees we observed the rays of the setting sun. Where the woods bordered a field, I stumbled over two large sacks of potatoes that seemed to have been concealed there for us. I had no doubt that they were a gift from heaven, and full of gratitude, we stuffed our pockets and sacks with this precious manna. It was a good sign.

We saw escaping Russians. Then suddenly there was excitement; revolver in hand, a soldier of the Wehrmacht approached us. He asked who we were and what we were doing, and after he had advised us not to build a fire in the woods, he went on his way. I was uneasy until he was out of sight. Our prison garb certainly attracted attention and did not make a favorable impression. It would be best for us to try to avoid all communities and to try to live in the woods until the arrival of the Allies.

However, if only we had had matches, we would have been able to cook the potatoes and ease our hunger. We needed matches, and we could not obtain them unless we asked the civilians for them. All evening, guided by the red rays of the setting sun, we trudged westward in search of our liberators. Noticing an isolated farm, we approached cautiously, hoping that the tenants would give us matches. As we neared the farmhouse, a dog barked menacingly; then a woman came out, followed stealthily by a soldier, perhaps a deserter. As politely as possible, I made my request. The woman responded that farther along we would find a large house where several of our comrades had already gathered and that someone would take care of us there. Thank you very much! We understood that no one here wanted to traffic with prisoners. Since we were not interested in having someone "to take care of us," we headed in the opposite direction. We preferred to go to sleep hungry.

We walked on, staying in the woods until night fell. Finally, at the end of our strength, we chose a thicket, rolled up in our blankets, and stretched out on a delightful bed of moss under a beautiful starry sky. It was a delectable night of delicate fragrances and other signs of spring. The preceding night we had still been in the power of the SS, but tonight here in the open we were awaiting the arrival of the Allies. Was it possible that two such different nights could fall in succession? As we asked God's help through an unknown tomorrow, how could we not thank Him, Who controlled our destiny, for today?

We drifted into peaceful sleep and awakened in an enchanted forest. What next? The plan was simple. We would go as far west as possible, try to learn where the front was, and find some matches. Still carrying our precious potatoes, courageously we resumed our march. But the sun went behind a cloud, and after a few hours I suspected that we were going in circles in this forest of full-grown trees. Coming upon a road, we carefully surveyed it for a moment; no one was traveling on it. We crossed it. On the other side were endless forests. We returned to the road. It at least led somewhere. In fact, a sign read "Gardelegen, 4 km." Imprudently, we decided to follow the road, for we needed both information and food. I stopped the first passing cyclist to ask him for matches, but he had none. We were luckier when the second cyclist promptly gave us matches and asked us why we were there and why we had been arrested. He cursed Hitler and his band, who had brought disaster on the country. He told us, furthermore, that the Americans were reported to be about thirty kilometers away, encircling the region, and that they might arrive that very evening. Then we hastily withdrew again into the woods, where we cooked our potatoes. We found a sheltered spot and with childish delight filled our soup tins with water from the forest stream. Then we boiled our potatoes and ate to our hearts' content.

Soon, the inescapable question arose again, "What next?" We did not feel that it was safe to wait here indefinitely. I was curious to know what was happening in the city. Since the approaching Americans would first occupy cities and towns, we wanted to make our way to a populated area. I had waited twenty-two months, but I felt the greatest impatience during the last hours! It seemed to us that, once we had escaped the claws of the SS, nothing very unfortunate could happen. How naïve we were!

Suddenly a shot rang out behind us. "Halt! Come here!" A soldier, who ordered us to follow him, led us about one hundred meters from where we were apprehended to a beautiful lodge surrounded by a park. We followed docilely, without any particular anxiety. Evidently, because of our prison garb and our vagabond appearance, he must have thought that we were terrorists. We did not make a favorable impression. Our suffering had taken its toll. There was a hardness in our face and our eyes were shifty.

The isolated lodge near the forest served as a field hospital. We were presented to an officer, a physician who was a captain. He was wearing many decorations. I read "Crete" on one, "African Corps" on another! He spoke French rather well. He questioned us at length to ask who we were, why we had been arrested, why we were there, and what our plans were. He seemed especially anxious to know whether or not any of the prisoners had been dangerous criminals. He was gentle, handsome, almost likable. He spoke to us politely, not in the condescending, brutal tones of the SS. Then a miracle happened. After he had told us reluctantly that he was going to turn us over to the police (he could not have suspected what we learned later—that thereby he would have sent us to certain death), he became sympathetic. He ordered for us a soup with meat in it, which we relished. Next we were given soap, a washcloth, and a razor, and we were allowed to bathe and shave at a spigot. Finally, a soldier brought each of us a clean white shirt. With astonishment and gratitude, we reveled in the simple pleasures of eating and bathing. There were, after all, some Germans who were human! I could not but think of Christ's words: "If ye then, being evil, know how to give good gifts . . . , how much more shall your Father which is in heaven give good things to them that ask him?" (Matt. 7:11).

We were given permission to remain in the park, where no one would harm us. We would be allowed to work if there were any tasks that we could perform. While we were waiting, we picked up the papers lying around the house. We wanted to be useful to show our gratitude and our good will.

Just then a soldier escorted in two Russians, escapees, like us, from our convoy. Their arrival disappointed us; we wanted to be the sole beneficiaries of our unexpected good fortune. The fact was that their arrival spoiled our luck, for the health officer could not extend the same hospitality when his yard was overrun with prisoners arrested in the woods.

The Russians, who stayed with us in a corner of the yard, were given food. I asked a soldier if he could supply us with civilian clothes. While he was looking for them, an officer warned us that we must leave immediately. We were to report to the city camp where our comrades were being housed. When the approaching Americans would arrive, we would be turned over to them. The city had been declared "open." Each of us received a box of canned food and some crackers, and in spite of our request to remain, we were obliged to leave.

Why this sudden change of attitude? Undoubtedly the officer had learned that the police and the SS were looking for escaped prisoners who would be classified as dangerous criminals, and he did not want to risk hiding us under the eyes of the SS. However, it is noteworthy that he did not deliver us to the police or assign a guard to escort us to the camp. He simply told us to leave.

One of the Russians protested that we would be killed. I admit that we were not very confident in the face of these new developments. We were torn by conflicting emotions. Amaro and I fell behind to let the Russians outdistance us. We would not see them again.

At the entrance of the city, some French prisoners of war approached us and all of them together warned us, "Get away fast, you guys; the police shoot at stripes. About twenty prisoners were shot today." Therefore, we returned to the woods. We were less confident than ever before. Our hearts pounded. We dreaded every encounter, and at every gunshot we suspected that someone was taking aim at us. Our legs felt heavy. Nevertheless, we urged ourselves on; we were not yet defeated. At the edge of the forest, investigating a sound in some bushes, I found the French doctor from Wieda, who also had fled. Before I could ask him why he remained in the thickets and what his plans were, he said, "Go anywhere except into the forest; it is full of soldiers." "Go anywhere" was easy to say, but there were not many hiding places. We were as frightened, famished, and exhausted as pursued beasts. Since it was late, we decided to spend the night in a dense thicket in the middle of a field. While we were approaching our place of refuge and preparing for sleep, we felt as if a thousand eyes were watching us. But perhaps this leafy island in the middle of the field could provide the best hiding place. After we had eaten the can of meat that had been given to us, we fell asleep. It was cold. From one direction, then another, rifle fire or the noise of moving tanks broke the silence of this night of unseen terrors. Finally, the day found us at the same spot. However, we were in a precarious position. If we had built a fire, we would have risked attracting attention. Therefore, after we had watched the edge of the woods for a long time and had observed no unusual activity, we abandoned our uncertain refuge and quickly took cover under the trees. We moved cautiously through the pines, the trunks of which provided only little protection. We met a rather shabbily dressed German, a poor devil who seemed to be digging for something. When I asked him if he had seen any soldiers, he replied that soldiers were everywhere and that he was an escaping prisoner. He showed us the striped trousers he was wearing under his civilian trousers. He seemed completely disoriented. This chance meeting added to our dilemma; we did not know what to do. The enemy was everywhere, invisible everywhere. A snapping branch was enough to startle us.

We changed direction. We saw nothing suspicious. Then in the distance through the trees we saw rings of blue smoke rising to play in the rays of the sun. Three silhouettes, perhaps those of woodcutters, crouched around the fire. As we approached, I was convinced that they also were prisoners; then I recognized a Russian from Osterhagen. He informed us that, like us, a whole convoy evacuated from Dora had escaped the night before. The SS and the civilian militia were hunting them. Much later we learned that this manhunt culminated in a massacre. The Russians advised us to keep going, not to skirt the woods, and not to penetrate too deeply. A nearby hollow seemed a suitable place at which to rest and to cook our potatoes. There, behind a curtain of trees, we stretched out for several hours. Still there was nothing unusual except occasional distant shots. How much longer would we have to wait? There was no indication that the front was moving toward us. Perhaps we were surrounded, but since this city was not strategic to the Americans, they had bypassed it. Therefore, we might need to hide out for a week or possibly two weeks.

We were very tense. On this April 13, I thought of my aunt who had reared me and whose birthday it was. I longed to see her again. Lord, help us; hasten the liberation of all those who otherwise would die!

This day would truly be for us the longest day of history. What would the day bring? How would we endure the growing burden of isolation in a hostile world?

Cautiously exploring our surroundings, we came upon a clearing in which there was a small, well-cared-for French cemetery, dating back to the Napoleonic wars. On the tombstone of one of my compatriots was the verse:

> They have lived their life
> They have cried their tears . . .

At a nearby intersection of forest trails, recently abandoned military equipment and packs led us to suspect that a retreating unit had passed through. We benefited from this windfall by taking whatever we could use—razors, soap, washcloths, paper; but we found nothing to eat. It would be better not to linger at this site. We returned to our hiding place and stretched out.

From a distance the city still presented the same enigmatic aspect. Shots from behind and from the side startled us, but we saw nothing. Trying to find shelter from which we could see without being seen, we traveled in circles in this immense forest. At times an unbearable silence, an indefinable oppression hung over the region as if some unalterable fate were snaring us in its web. By what similar secretive premonitions does death warn the living of her approach?

What ominous dread seized our thoughts! Unanswerable questions sapped our fortitude. We were shipwrecked and trapped in a sinking vessel. We were caught in the quicksands of anguish. Had we struggled for two years (and what a two years!) only to be vanquished this close to the end? Such an outcome would be absurd. But war is absurd!

Toward noon, we cooked our last potatoes. However, we no longer enjoyed them without salt; in fact, I suspect that they had been nipped by the frost. We were completely disheartened.

Then events followed in rapid succession. I can only summarize what happened, but, Lord, how long the hours were!

When Amaro decided to find out what was happening at the edge of the forest, I stretched out to await his return. A half hour, an hour, two hours, maybe three hours passed. What was he doing? I began to imagine all sorts of mishaps. It was not like him to cause me concern. I began to look for him, and I searched the whole area that we had covered together. Thinking that he might be trying to take more loot, I returned to the scattered sacks of clothing. While I was contemplating these once-proud military uniforms now scornfully cast aside, suddenly I held my breath at the sight of two soldiers sleeping a short distance away. I dared not move. However, they had not heard me. They looked peaceful, and they were unarmed. From the half-opened mouth of one trickled a thin stream of blood. I approached. They were not long dead. I hurried away from this disquieting spot—forward, forward with no backward glance. It was perhaps 5:00 P.M. Still no trace of Amaro! What had happened to him? If he had been killed, I would have found his body. Had he lost his mind and run away? Anything was possible in our predicament. I was literally overwhelmed with emotion. To pass within three days from the heights of joy to the valley of death was more than our frailty could endure. My nerves were on edge; they had been stretched to their limit. I had to face the fact that my companion had disappeared and I did not know what had happened to him. I was seized by anguish as I faced the prospect of being absolutely alone. I was feeling my way through the shadows of Good Friday. At that time, I could not know that I was about to emerge into the light of the Resurrection.

In this hostile country, only the Public Health soldiers who had welcomed me the previous evening had demonstrated any human warmth. They were my only hope. Taking my knapsack and blanket and leaving those of Amaro in case he should return, I made my way through the woods and soon came upon the path. Confusion reigned in the park. The staff seemed to be evacuating. When the officer noticed me, he called, "Well, there you are again." I explained that I had not come to ask for charity. I wanted only to be allowed to stay in the park. Everywhere else the police were shooting escapees, and several of my comrades had been killed. I was not a criminal and I did not want to die. The officer was sympathetic. When he asked where my friend was, I replied, "Kaputt," and my answer seemed to touch him. He said, "Stay in the park. No one will bother you." I was overwhelmed with gratitude. The soldiers were very busy, but I paid no attention to them. A sergeant who noticed me gave me a pack of cigarettes. I did not know how to thank him. A little later he brought me five packets of combat rations. Each contained cigarettes, chocolate, and biscuits. His kindness was more than I could have expected from an unknown German, and I was on the verge of tears. Because of these anonymous acts of mercy, which the benefactors would surely forget in the tumult that accompanied the end of the war, I would be able to forgive much suffered at the hands of the Germans.

I quickly regained happiness. I was ecstatic. I was given two kilograms of fresh bread, margarine, two cans of meat, a tin of fish, and even a bottle of champagne—from Reims! And only a few minutes ago I had been famished! Now I had enough food for a week in the woods. My confidence restored, I no longer thought of past dangers. Life overcame despair.

I quickly ate some biscuits and set about finding clothing more suitable than my prison stripes. I was given trousers, a jacket, and a pullover. Now, aside from my shaved head, I bore no signs of a conscripted laborer. A soldier informed me that tonight I would sleep in a bed. I tried to fathom the mysteries of the German soul. While I was trying on a pair of shoes, I heard very loud shouts, the clatter of machine gun fire, and the noise of scurrying feet. All the soldiers ran outside with their hands over their heads. Thinking that the matter did not involve me, I continued to put on my precious shoes. I could hardly believe my eyes, but somebody was pointing a gun at me. I, too, had to run outside with my hands raised.

They were indeed Americans, with American helmets, American jeeps, the American star! My legs trembled. I wanted to give some sign of friendship, but they did not appear to understand. They drove us at double time back to the road, where I was loaded along with the Germans into a truck. I had to leave behind the food I had hardly tasted. What difference did it make now? The army trucks sped along through clouds of dust. Like a whirlwind, we flew through villages where groups of foreign prisoners were saluting their liberators. Finally, about forty kilometers from the forest lodge, the trucks rolled to a stop at nightfall. We were led into the courtyard of a large farm. Frisking, interrogation! I declared that I was French. "Oh, French!" I was led to the Military Police, and from then on I was a free man. I lodged with the soldiers in their quarters. These long-legged boys were likable, straightforward in their relationships, not loudmouths like our former guards. I ate

American chocolate and smoked Luckies. I was so intoxicated with joy that I could not sleep. I could not be sure whether my dream was coming true or whether I was still dreaming. When we long await and earnestly yearn for the fulfillment of a fantasy, we dare not believe that our desire is being realized.

Nevertheless, my joy was not complete. I was thinking about Amaro, who must have died only a few hours before the liberation we had fervently wished to experience together. Even the brightest joys are clouded, as I realized when I returned to France and learned of the casualties in my family.

About a month later, in France, I found Amaro, miraculously still alive. He explained what had happened. After he had left me, he was arrested only a short distance away by a German patrol. He had spoken loudly to try to alert me, but I had heard nothing, and I had seen nothing; yet I do not remember dozing. It was a miracle that I was not arrested also. Amaro found himself captive with two Russians. At any moment they expected to be dispatched by a bullet in the back of the neck. They were escorted back to Gardelegen and placed once again in the hands of the SS. By the evening of April 13, the Americans had not penetrated into Gardelegen; instead, their columns had simply bypassed the city. Although the Americans were around and beyond the city, during the night the SS corralled all the prisoners who had been recaptured and herded them into a large barn. There were perhaps twelve hundred, of whom two hundred were French. There surely were some there whose fate no one would ever know. There was straw in the barn. Machine guns were trained on all the exits. The German prisoners were called out, and the Polish prisoners exited with them. The Germans and the Poles were given guns with which to prevent the escape of their "foreign" comrades. Then the SS tried to ignite the straw with burning newspapers, but each time the prisoners extinguished the flames. Next the SS threw incendiary grenades; the barn kindled and became a torch. Frightful screams issued from this gigantic holocaust. Those who rushed for the exits were shot, but it was better to die from a bullet than to be burned alive. Amaro was near a door when a machine gun was fired only a few inches away on his left. The bodies of the poor victims fell against him and formed a wall that briefly protected him from the flames. The SS, certain that no one had escaped, fled. Then Amaro, literally wild, dragged himself out. He told me that, of twelve hundred men, not more than ten escaped from the furnace. The Americans entered the city in the morning. The barn was still smoldering, and they discovered one thousand sixteen charred corpses. This final crime, hardly believable, bears the stamp of nazism!

A few days later, I read in an American journal an illustrated report of this incident. It has been confirmed that Himmler had ordered the concentration camp commandants to exterminate the prisoners and to destroy the evidence. Such was the goal of the Nazi system; such were the demoniac excesses. The proof of the evil has been provided for all time if mankind does not choose to have a short memory.

During the next few days, not wanting always to remain with the Military Police, I cultivated an acquaintance with a group of French prisoners of war, and I attached myself to their commando. About forty of us lodged in a large room. Gradually I learned again to act like a free person. I wore an American military jacket, and I carried a high-caliber pistol I had found, but it was not loaded. This impersonation made it easier to "arrange for" food. In the confusion, supplies were not arriving, and it became necessary to scrounge for provisions. The farmers were not unwilling to give us bacon, sausage, milk, and potatoes. We were polite, and I noticed that my German vocabulary learned in the concentration camps had a persuasive effect. I ate everything that I could find, but it took two weeks of overeating to satisfy my hunger. For the first few days, without provoking more than a mild disorder, I ate the meat spreads directly from the can, and I added powdered milk to fresh milk. My stomach was like iron. Only the insane would eat to such excess, but I was mad for food! I rapidly gained weight.

However, during these last few days we were waiting impatiently to see again our family and friends. We had to wait until the military authorities could reestablish communications. In Germany there were millions of foreigners waiting for repatriation. The truth about Buchenwald was reported over the radio. What would my relatives think? They had not heard from me for ten months.

We were living among the German people, upon whom an unprecedented catastrophe had fallen. All shops had been ransacked, and already the breadlines were forming. In the villages there were daily eyewitness accounts of acts of vengeance by former Russian prisoners against the Nazis. The Germans were pathetic in defeat; without a leader, they were helpless. Those who had formerly paraded boisterously were now creeping about like mice.

At the end of April we left Gross-Schwarzlosen and went to Stendal. Three days later, we went by American army truck to the Hildesheim Air Base. Already I was ecstatically anticipating the flight home. However, I was registered as a political prisoner; the prisoners of war were given priority. It was annoying that the Americans treated the liberated conscripted laborers as civilians! I was directed to a small camp where all sorts of deportees, S.T.O. conscriptees, volunteers, and even collaborators were assembled. I found some fellow inmates, and immediately we became friends. Two days later, we were transferred to Hannover, a beautiful city now in ruins. We left on a night train. With thirty persons to a cattle car, we were less uncomfortable than we had been in other transports. The trip was long. Everywhere the rails were being repaired. All the way to the Rhine, not a single station remained standing. This country had been utterly destroyed. It took us three days to cross Germany. At last, on May 7, we arrived in Holland.

Here the scenery changed. There was no obvious destruction. On a hill flew the Dutch flag. We were so happy to leave the cursed German soil that we saluted the Dutch flag with shouts of joy. We were entering friendly territory. Just at that moment the announcement was made on the radio that an armistice had been signed. A huge flag hung from every window. Everyone was in a holiday mood. From our car we could see the crowd that poured into the streets for the victory celebration. As soon as people noticed our flag-draped train, they ran toward us. Children threw flowers, girls threw kisses, old people wept. We witnessed scenes of the greatest joy even in the smallest hamlets. Everywhere there were shouts of joy. Everyone made the V-for-Victory sign. There was delirium. I was so over-whelmed that tears rolled down my cheeks. I wanted to embrace everyone in the world.

At midnight we arrived in the Maastricht station. While we were being served a warm bouillon, a group of young people crowded onto the platform and danced the farandole. Nobody was sleeping when we crossed into Belgium. Liège and Namur, flag-bedecked, welcomed us in our mother tongue.

And the journey continued, enlivened by the enthusiasm of those from whom the nightmare of war was receding. About 10:00 A.M. on May 8, our train crossed into France. Givet, the first French sta-tion, a dear little town, was a symbol of our rediscovered native land. If we had not suffered far from France, we would not have known how much we loved her. Some nuns rushed toward us, then Red Cross workers with milk, bouillon, and, best of all, the sustain-ing assurance that France had not forgotten us.

By early afternoon, we were in Charleville, where the formalities of repatriation were completed. Here we were given special consid-eration; those who had been deported were given priority. I pointed out to Military Security a German who was trying to gain entry under false identification. At 3:00 P.M., standing under the shower, I heard the victory speech of General de Gaulle as it was broadcast over a loudspeaker. A nurse carefully attended to my boils, which were still draining. Then an elderly lady, who wanted to express kindness, insisted that some of us go to her home for refreshments. Good and cordial people of the North!

There were flags everywhere, strains of the Marseillaise, uni-forms, smiling girls, a resplendent sun, wine—the first in two years—and the express train to Marseille. The atmosphere was charged on this official V-Day. I snatched up French newspapers; I craved information. As the train went through the stations, again we saw flags, and charming young women offered us wine and swirled through the farandole before a backdrop of the flowering countryside. My head was spinning! At each station the scene was repeated: there were hundreds of searching eyes, uncontrollably emotional reunions, and bitter disappointment for those whose loved one did not disembark.

Lyon, Valence, our Rhone River valley! I spent the night in Avignon. May 10 at 9:00 A.M., the train entered Nîmes. My telegram had arrived. A moment of hesitation, then arms outstretched! What joy to find ourselves together after many dark hours of separation! What sadness also to learn of the losses during my absence! Like an ignited fuse, the news spread: Aimé has returned! All of our friends came running. Yes, of course, I had changed!

The countryside around Nîmes sprawled under a glorious sun. The first grasshoppers were already performing. Life went on with the usual pains and joys. Would not the grass grow thick and green through the ruins? Would not life also prevail?

We must believe in life. We must love life. We must be committed to life.

Epilogue

I have just written my memoirs. I have filled page after page before the memories could escape me or become vague. I have written them to relieve myself, in one sense, from a burden. But to whom should I confide such reminiscences? "If we should survive, who will believe our report," we used to ask ourselves; "and why would the SS permit to survive a single telltale witness to so many crimes?"

Indeed, of our prison convoy of 1,200 from Compiègne, given inmate numbers from 20,000, how many returned? Maybe thirty or forty—certainly no more—3 or 4 percent at the most. It was not the fault of the SS that so many returned! Furthermore, some of the survivors were in such poor health that it was doubtful that they would ever recover. All of us had experienced too much nutritional deficiency, exposure, and physical exhaustion in sordid conditions to avoid permanent damage. We had aged at least twenty years.

Therefore, some of us must rouse ourselves to speak. We must speak for those who did not return and who will never again be heard here. However, we must force ourselves to this effort; we hardly enjoy speaking out. We must constrain ourselves to unlock the dark secret buried in our flesh and in our spirit. We owe this testimony to our friends, to all those faces that we still envision. How can we forget our companions, our beloved brothers who died too soon? The memory of them haunts us and pursues us. Above the glades of the German forests, it rises in acrid clouds from the crematories. Like lingering shadows, it pervades the cell blocks. It wafts through the tunnels and through the barracks and hovers over the assembly yard, over the quarries, and over all the places where our comrades struggled alone against death.

However, with the inadequate words at our command, how can we describe our ordeal, the total experience of all the contributing hardships? Should we speak of the demented world of the concentration camp or of the endless abandonment while time stood still? It has been clear to me from the beginning how difficult it would be to communicate our experience. Now, when I think, "But, finally, that time has passed; it is over and done," I know indeed that I am still back there, even though I am not there in the same sense in which I was there formerly.

As I have already said, our true misery is difficult to perceive. Any given incident, described in two lines, might seem insignificant if it appeared along with a description of other incidents. Nevertheless, such a single given incident might reveal the height of suffering that can be endured at any given moment.

I know that I have reported only a small part of what happened to us and that I am understating the reality. I do not want to enumerate endless details or without restraint to expose all the corruption. The reading of such a report would be intolerable. For example, should I fully describe the scene in which Schmidt harassed a homosexual by forcing him at gunpoint to masturbate in front of the whole camp assembly? Or should I describe how Schmidt brutally beat an Italian and left him lying on the assembly yard, where he suffered for three days before he died? Or should I describe how Schmidt maliciously hosed down a Russian commando, forced to stand at attention while the water froze? There would be no end to attempting to recall the daily horror that we knew.

Only a rare literary talent could create the reality of this hell. How can the written word describe it? The reality of the human drama always defies description.

What is the lesson of the ordeal? If suffering and death, as exemplified by our experience, do not enable us to formulate a rule of conduct, we must despair! Of course, life goes on; we must look to the future, but not as if there has been no past. Have we experienced the extravagant privilege of survival only to conclude, "Henceforth, let us eat and drink, for tomorrow we shall die"? If we drew this conclusion, we would be unworthy of survival.

However, what can we add that would be neither banal nor pedantic? People make such remarks to me as, "You have had some very unusual experiences; as you reflect, surely these experiences will take on new meaning." They simply do not understand the extent to which our lives were burning out, like a spark feeding on the last drop of physical existence and of existence beyond the physical. Our lives were only a spark. We were not enriched by our ordeal, but as a result of our experience, we perceive more clearly what we should cultivate and defend. We were stripped of all our usual security and social amenities, and thus we learned to discern what is essential.

This lesson is for everybody, for the Nazis perpetrated their crimes against humanity. The civilized world was shocked by reports about the Third Reich's "death houses": Buchenwald, Auschwitz, Mauthausen, Ravensbrück, Dachau, Bergen-Belsen, Oranienburg, Sachsenhausen, Struthof, etc., etc. The Nazi regime organized these forced labor camps on a systematic, extensive, scientific scale and introduced into them a degree of cruelty and abuse never before experienced in the countries of Western civilization. It would be necessary to delve deep into history, into periods of dark barbarity, to discover a comparable refinement of the art of exterminating human beings. The Nazis made extermination a political goal and derived pleasure from watching their victims suffer.

The responsibility of the German people is most disconcerting. I understand that many now say that they were unaware of what was happening. Memory is so conveniently selective! Is it true that they did not know? Probably not all knew of the frightful treatment of those sent to the camps, but there were many Germans who were all too well informed. Did not the civilians whom we met know? The representatives of large corporations, who exploited us as slaves, often sniggered when the SS bludgeoned us. Oh, the unfathomable evasions of the German soul! "It is a mountain of sins and crimes which rises before us, now that the fog of deceitful propaganda has dissipated. And the horror of our crimes is so great that none of us dares to look it in the face, and each tries to close his eyes as if it were a dream" (Martin Niemöller, *The German Guilt*). It frightens me that among those who seemed shocked that such incidents took place in their country, a majority brought Hitler to power, desired his victory, and would have covered up the crimes perpetrated to ensure a thousand-year domination by the master race. If Hitler is renounced today, he is renounced because he was defeated. "When Pastor Niemöller entered a concentration camp in 1937, this date was recorded as that of the beginning of concentration camps, but these camps existed already in 1933; and those who were being sent there were the Communists. Who worried about them? We were informed, nevertheless; their imprisonment was reported in the newspapers. Then the disabled, the so-called incurables, were liquidated. The persecution of the Jews and our behavior in occupied territories were reported in the newspapers. Because a few individuals committed acts of sabotage, hundreds of hostages were executed" (ibid.).

Depraved individuals are to be found everywhere. Of course, I understand the economic, political, and social causes that explain the rise of nazism in Germany, but how could nazism find thousands and thousands of men for a police force of blindly criminal character. Indeed, I have never encountered a single member of the SS who was not a criminal. I do not know what accounts these criminals will be required to settle with God, but I believe that in terms of human justice it would be criminal negligence some day to exonerate these culprits as if nothing had ever happened. Ah! We are not proposing that we treat them as they treated us. We do not want vengeance; we want justice and a measure of decency. And most of all we want never again to witness what has been! We do not seek vengeance against the German people, but we seek to help them cast out their demons, of which militarism is one of the most tenacious. What we have learned from the struggle of the Confessing Church and from its many unknown supporters who under unusual duress resisted Hitler's demoniac program inspires true hope. "Peradventure ten righteous shall be found there, will You, nevertheless destroy the city?" (Gen. 18 : 32).

Our ordeal revealed the true face of nazism and of all systems based on contempt for the individual. Well-researched studies of such systems have long been available, and we can become informed by reading these publications. The trouble is that no one has taken them seriously. "We shall see!" Alas, one sees too late. Nazism established a method by which a sixteen-year-old boy was trained to be a torturer and a hangman. The ideal he set for himself was that of service in the world of the concentration camp.

The concentration camp re-created a primitive society in which the strong crushed the weak in the struggle for life. At the same time the camp safeguarded such outward manifestations of civilized society as the authority of the law. *Jedem das Seine* (to each his rights) was wrought in Buchenwald's main gate. In fact, "justice," "order," "law," were made to serve the camp officials. Theft for their profit was always permitted; otherwise, stealing was punished by death.

We conquered the Nazis militarily, but did we conquer nazism? Nazism is absolute evil, the power of demons who lurk in the hearts of all human beings and who wait only to discover receptive spirits over which to cast their spell. Henceforth, we must not tolerate disrespect for any person anywhere; we must not permit anyone to be hungry, to be brutalized by the police, to be committed to a degrading penitentiary, to become only a number in the blind cogs of economic interests. Nor can we permit racist propaganda to be freely disseminated.

After the terrible shock experienced in our country, we must unsparingly exert ourselves to rebuild, for France has a function in the community of nations. Certainly, we have learned that exaggerated national pride leads to idolatry. Nevertheless, in exile we thought continuously of our native land; we became acutely aware that our homeland is irreplaceable and that every individual needs to nurture his roots. Consequently, we are compelled to safeguard our heritage. In spite of ideological diversities, we agree fundamentally on the essential, on a humanism engendered, consciously or unconsciously, by Christian values. We desire a country in which the institutions will allow us to expand and fulfill our destiny in our own communities. We want a country that practices moderation and justice, that defends liberty and promotes brotherhood. Furthermore, we must work passionately for peace, because peace is never definitively achieved. Each individual can work wherever he finds himself; he can begin by becoming aware of his neighbor, by cultivating through dialogue his relationship with others, by ensuring that no system, ideologies, or myths will ever destroy this relationship. To this end we must educate our youth. Thus perhaps we shall spare our children the horror of the concentration camps. At least we shall—indeed, we must—spare them from becoming hangmen, even if we cannot save them from becoming martyrs.

Our ordeal was for us a moment-by-moment struggle in which we were engaged body and soul. Every minute we were obliged to resist the overall oppression rather than to concentrate on any single hardship, for no aspect of our condition was insignificant. I was in good health when I was arrested, but my initial well-being could not prevail against the overwhelming degradation that preyed upon us. Those who survived the longest were those who struggled, who willed, who hoped.

In this form of resistance, our culture, our ethics, our faith, were not hypothetical; they were essential elements of our will to live. These elements morally fortified but at the same time made vulnerable those who did not believe that the end justifies the means. Often, as my comrades fell under the blows of their tormentors, I thought that the victims were like those of whom the apostle spoke—those who "had trial of cruel mockings and scourgings, yea, moreover of bonds and imprisonment: They were stoned, they were sawn asunder, were tempted, were slain with the sword: they wandered about in sheepskins and goatskins; being destitute, afflicted, tormented; (Of whom the world was not worthy)" (Heb. 11:36–38).

Contrary to what one might expect, solidarity for resisting was found only within small groups. From the outset we experienced difficulty in creating a climate for understanding and trust among the various nationality groups. It was by succeeding in promoting enmities through the organization, regimentation, and mixing of prisoners of various categories (not all Resistance prisoners, alas!) that creators of the concentration camps fully demonstrated their genius. The relentless struggle for survival aggravated our natural distrust of one another. The most insignificant incident could provoke a quarrel. This jealous self-interest was not the least of our moral weaknesses. I cannot emphasize strongly enough that frightful evidence demonstrated to us that man is a wolf to man, that he is naturally not altruistic but egotistic and that all of us are guilty.

Our whole existence was caught up in this drama, and I realized that I must face the conflict and accept my destiny, because God mysteriously permitted that I be in a concentration camp as He had previously permitted that I be in prison and at Compiègne. "Thou crushest me, Lord, but it is sufficient for me to recognize Thy hand" (Calvin). We can preserve life only at the risk of losing it. For many of my comrades this time of imprisonment was worthless; it was lost time taken from their best years. Who did not yearn for the end? However, in the eyes of God, there is no lost time; there is no wasted time. He is the master of time; He fills it and gives it meaning.

We experienced human distress. To the last hour, we were spared nothing. Certainly, many others have suffered as much as we, and not only because of war! However, we, the deported, stood at the center of the tragedy. "There is no comparison between the fate of the soldier and the fate of the hostage" (Saint-Exupéry). In this monstrous undertaking of dehumanization, some outstanding figures emerged like Albert, Georges, Lorentz—a young French Christian, a Czechoslovakian socialist, an old German communist. I cannot mention their names without feeling a great sense of gratitude. Others, elsewhere, can also evoke such names. There is a permanence in the humanity of man—despite attempts at dehumanization—that restores our courage and hope. Certainly we do not wish to present ourselves as heroes, and if the manner in which some were obliged to set their example can serve as witness, the heroism was not of a form that we would have chosen. We persevered because it was necessary to persevere. For me, all strength came from above.

It has been said that suffering is a source of our inner freedom. The statement is rash. Suffering refines or embitters us; it hardens our souls or renders them receptive to grace. Frequently, our attitude toward suffering is, at the same time, one of rejection and of acceptance. In any case, suffering does not leave us as we were. We can neither welcome nor take pleasure in suffering, but, when it is present, we must confront it and overcome it. Suffering should elevate us. We must recognize that true freedom is revealed through the suffering of Christ, for our suffering was lifted at the cross.

In desperate situations, I experienced the true presence of Christ and the power of faith. "If God *be* for us, who *can be* against us?" (Rom. 8:31). Deprived of all security, of all religious shibboleths learned by habit, new power was given to us through the ability to believe that His grace is sufficient.

We learned anew to pray. Of course, it is natural to cry "help" when we are in trouble! However, we truly learned anew the prayer of intercession and the prayer of gratitude. We experienced the effectiveness of universal communion as we felt ourselves uplifted by the prayer of the Church, by the prayers of those far away who interceded for us. I am speaking here in the name of many Christians, both Catholic and Protestant, who too seldom have shared such moments of special grace. In the future, believers throughout the world should dedicate themselves to pray for those who no longer are able to pray or for those who no longer know how to pray.

From a human point of view, we should not have survived. Some of us have been given another chance. Should we preach hatred and seek the fleeting satisfaction of vengeance? No, we must oppose alienation and the contagion of hatred. Personally, I know that God allowed me to survive to bear witness to his love and reconciliation. But how can I love my enemy? This formidable question is addressed to our generation. True pardon is not achieved by forgetting or weakening or retreating but rather by a committed, collective effort against evil. We must discover the real person despite the blindly evil character that he plays. Such a course is difficult. It demands that we exceed our human possibilities, but we are led by our Lord, who loved with the hope that enabled him to say at the culmination of His suffering, "Father, forgive them . . ."

For me it has become important to labor to edify this people of a church composed of men who know themselves to be small, suffering, guilty, threatened, but who have found in the Gospel new reasons to live. Our consecration to Him does not exclude involvement with the affairs of this world, but they are secondary. We know that the key for the dramatic history of this world was revealed on the hill of Golgotha when the Son of Man was hanged on a cross and when by His obedience He destroyed all the powers of darkness. We know also that all the despair of this world cannot invalidate the great hope of a "new heaven and a new earth where justice will reign."

Appendix

Deportees and Christianity in the Nazi Concentration Camps

It was as a young Frenchman and as a Christian that I personally, from 1940 on, leaned toward the Resistance. Spiritual motivation—the Huguenot tradition of resistance to oppression, Bible reading, the influence of the theologian Karl Barth, the alarm signal of anti-Semitism—played an essential role in determining my inclination.

One of the problems of conscience that presented itself to us as Christians then was that of the use of violence. A draft dodger with respect to the S.T.O. (Le Service du Travail Obligatoire en Allemagne [the Service of Compulsory Labor]), I could have tried to cross into Switzerland to pursue theological studies to which I felt called, but such a move would have seemed to me to suggest escapism. In the tragedy that was striking so many people in our country and in Europe in general, there was no longer a place for an attitude of merely spiritual support, nonviolence, wait-and-see. As Jacques Monod, upon joining the Maquis, declared to his friends of the Christian Students Federation, in a letter that jolted us, the time for total commitment had come: "I am leaving without hatred, convinced that we, Christians, have no right to allow only the unbelievers to sacrifice their lives."[1]

This testimony necessarily evokes certain personal experiences.

1. Jacques Monod, Professor of Letters at Marseille, was killed in a Maquis battle at Chaudesaigues, Cantal, June 20, 1944.
"Deportees and Christianity in the Nazi Concentration Camps" from *Eglises et chetiens dans la IIe guerre* (Presses Universitaires de Lyon, 1978). Republished with permission.

But I am convinced that I am voicing what was experienced by most of our comrades who conscientiously adhered to Christianity and of whom the majority no longer exists to bear witness. Yet I am fully aware of the difficulty of communicating such an experience.

Suffice it to characterize the concentration camps as a nightmare universe. The Nazi regime and its fanatical supporters knowingly plunged us into an abyss of suffering, scorn, and degradation. In this system, manifestations of any kind of religious life were strictly prohibited. The Buchenwald signpost pointing to SS barracks in one direction and prisoner quarters in another bore wooden sculptings of a priest, a Jew, a Communist, and a black-market agent, thereby eloquently identifying the enemies of the regime. In the convoys that brought the prisoners to the camps, the priests distinguished by their cassocks were especially mistreated.

Nevertheless, following an agreement between the Holy See and the Third Reich, priests were congregated at Dachau where they were exempted from heavy work.[2] The French priests thus saved by the Vatican intervention from a more tragic winter arrived at Dachau in the autumn of 1944 from Mauthausen and Buchenwald.

2. This order of the Nazi Central Office for the Security of the Reich can be dated as of October 16, 1944. The measure was implemented during December 1944 and January 1945, when ecclesiastics held in other concentration camps were transported to Dachau.

The order coincides with an intervention of the Holy See through the pope's representative in Berlin, Orsenigo, who was instructed to make an appeal on behalf of the French deportees (telegram from Tardini, October 11, 1944, no. 914). This intervention, confirmed in November by an anonymous note, was pursuant to Abbé Rodhain's arrival in Rome, where Rodhain was sent by Cardinal Suhard to plead the cause of French and Belgian deportees.

Orsenigo's role as permanent representative merits a closer examination. A very controversial figure (highly appreciated by Pius XI but held in low esteem by Pius XII), he was "retired" immediately after Liberation. This negotiation with German authorities became known only through the brief telegram.

Edmond Michelet, long-term minister of the de Gaulle government, has described the religious activity that inevitably ensued despite the restrictions:

In block 26, occupied by German clerics, two rooms had been transformed into a chapel. Mass was celebrated there every morning, but admission was denied to everybody outside the block. Block 28 was occupied by Polish priests. These had no more access to the chapel than had we, the laity. If it occurred to anyone of the Poles to venture in, he was expelled—sometimes with fisticuffs: I have witnessed them. Thus it was that, beside the pitiful spectacle that the enslaved Church of block 26 presented, the suffering Church of block 28 stood in contrast because of the comfort that she offered. Here, we breathed what must have been the atmosphere of the catacombs under Diocletian. The secret, pre-dawn Sunday masses, in overcrowded chambers, the enslaved laborers with drawn features, a derisible iron goblet substituting for a chalice, a lozenge box for a poor ciboire containing the miniscule host, the priest prudently officiating in his everyday rags without the least liturgical ornamentation—all that had an extraordinary appeal, a gripping majesty. At each end of the barrack, a comrade stood guard to make sure that no SS would come, in an excess of zeal, to disturb the nocturnal ceremony, as had been done many times lately, not without carnage. When a Christian, whatever his nationality, was recognized by one of the Polish priests, he was fraternally invited to partake of the Eucharistic feast of block 28. . . . It was only when our French parish priests began to police the door of the reserved enclosure themselves that, progressively, the immoderate restriction was relaxed; then admission to the chapel became open to almost anyone. . . . In the chapel, standing pressed against each other, five or six hundred priests silently followed the celebrant's prayers. . . . Different confessions shared block 26 and the chapel. The Catholic clergy was more numerous, but there were also many Reform pastors, a certain number of Orthodox priests, mostly from Yugoslavia or Romania, and even a marabout from Albania.[3]

Even a sacerdotal ordination, that of a German deacon, Karl Leistner, was planned in the greatest secrecy and celebrated by Monsignor Piguet, bishop of Clermont-Ferrand, on December 17, 1944.[4]

On Christmas Eve of 1944, after seven and a half years of incarceration as "the Führer's personal prisoner," Pastor Martin Niemöller obtained for the first time authorization to conduct a monthly service for his fellow Protestant prisoners in the military headquarters jail at the camp of Dachau. His sermon notes were published for the avowed purpose "of attesting that in the midst of these days of terror, the Gospel has remained for us the power of God."[5]

For various reasons not all the priests or pastors were at Dachau. I knew about ten of them at Buchenwald and in the commandos in which I found myself, and in general—there are always exceptions—I fully subscribe to this evaluation:

The religious leaders, priests or pastors, were admirably stoic, ill favored by the SS and the German prisoners; dispossessed of their religious articles, they remained no less conscience guides for their fellow sufferers. Hearing confessions, giving communion in the greatest secrecy, they were for all a great comfort.[6]

I want to express also the infinite gratitude that I feel personally for men like Pastor Marcel Heuzé, Pastor Henri Orange, Abbé Amyot, Father Georges.

3. Edmond Michelet, *Rue de la Liberté*, pp. 114–17.
4. François Goldschmit, "Le Bon Dieu en KZ," in *Alsaciens-Lorrains à Dachau*, Sarreguemines, 1946–47.
5. Martin Niemöller, *Cellule 34* (Geneva: Labor & Fides, 1947).
6. René G. Marnot, *Dix-huit mois au bagne de Buchenwald* (Tours: 1945).

But obviously we must not limit Christianity to the ecclesiastics. It is an established fact that the Christian faith constituted for many prisoners one of the essential wellsprings of their resistance. Moral resistance, to preserve the human being from renunciation or from degradation, demanded a much greater effort than resistance to physical conditions, which was no small matter. It is undeniable that those who held out best were those who had a faith, an ideal— religious, political, or simply humanistic. It was popularly stated that "Communist or religious women endured because the one and the other group had a faith."[7]

But it is difficult to say where the Christian attitude starts and ends, to evaluate the importance of faith and the role that it played for the prisoners in the situation that was theirs. Here we are on a subjective plain, and it is not ours to sound the heart and soul; for some, the attitude also depended on place, circumstance, and the influence of this or that comrade.

If the Christian presence in the concentration camps is a reality not to be underestimated, it is noteworthy that nowhere to our knowledge was there a true organized body of Christians; indeed, only the "invisible Church" could exist. At most there were small prayer groups and mutual aid groups. Furthermore, Christians and non-Christians were subjected to the same hardships and practiced solidarity in the same battle that together they waged, "he who believed in heaven and he who believed not,"[8] according to Aragon's famous words.

How then was the Christian witness conveyed?

Perhaps in the first place we must emphasize that it was incarnate in certain admirable and incontestably Christian figures who, through the asceticism that was imposed on us, attained true saintliness.

No doubt, speaking of saints, we must name the blessed Father

7. Marie-Elisa Nordmann-Cohen, *Témoignage sur Auschwitz.*
8. *La Rose et le Réséda.*

Maximilien Kolbe, a Pole, who voluntarily took the place of the father of a family, Francis Gajowniczek, condemned to die of starvation in an Auschwitz bunker. The Catholic church has since canonized Father Kolbe. What an exemplary attitude of a transparent love, which goes to the limits of the agape logic!

But not all the saints are lifted up onto the altars. Many acts of charity and of abnegation, truly heroic in the conditions under which they occurred, were executed without witnesses. We must add that if our remarks here concern those motivated by the Christian faith, there were also "atheist saints," or those who called themselves atheists, who tried to promote solidarity, to save lives, to oppose the SS death wish at the risk of losing their own lives. Those, likewise, we will not forget.

The survivors' reports quite often cite these persons who were striking because of the quality of their humanity and their moral radiance; for example:

> You, Yvonne Baratte, radiant as an archangel in your ridiculous robe, you knew how to say the very simple word whose force, come from above, transfigures all sorrows; you who have paid with your life for the gift that you gave to your sisters. And Mado Bonouvrier, also dead of a devotion that went to foolishness, to the foolishness of saints. . . . We have survived these hours because, among us, despite disagreements and grumblings, and sometimes villanies that might have destroyed our inner life forces, a flame was burning in beings of pure charity which we did not need to have pointed out to us: we felt a radiance at their approach. . . . He is a saint—this Nanouk who leads the Protestant service as Yvonne leads the Catholic prayers. Each instant of his life is a gift of himself. . . . Now that several months have passed since our frightful adventure, what remains outstanding from these scenes of terror, like a precious stone in the middle of a slough, is the miracle of charity which these

exceptional beings—at the price of such effort as we shall never know how to exert—made glow in our shadows, where thanks to them the Eternal visited us.[9]

Germaine Tillion, in an Association of Deportees bulletin, gave a similar report of Henriette Roux at Ravensbrück (the wife of Pastor Roux, also deported from Marseille).

And Corrie Ten Boom, the Dutch woman so confident in the power of her Lord, had the courage to seize on certain opportunities to witness. One day, she engaged an especially cruel guard in dialogue:

> "Till now you have been a curse upon us: the Lord can make you a blessing."
>
> "That's impossible at Ravensbrück. This is hell!"
>
> "Yes, it's hell. But do you know that the greatest danger to which you're exposed here is that of losing your soul?"[10]

At Mauthausen, Father Jacques spent himself without reserve to help his comrades, Catholic or not, materially and spiritually; he was one of the individuals held in high regard.[11]

The German theologian Dietrich Bonhoeffer, implicated in the plot against Hitler and incarcerated in Berlin, then at Buchenwald, was hanged in the concentration camp of Flossenbürg on April 9, 1945. Since the end of the war, his writings in captivity have had a considerable influence on European theology. The appreciation of his few companions in captivity for his character is unanimous. The camp doctor at Flossenbürg wrote:

9. Yvonne Pagniez, *Scènes de la vie du bagne* (Flammarion, 1947), pp. 134, 163, 195.

10. Corrie Ten Boom, *Victoire à Ravensbrück* (Geneva: 1974), p. 156.

11. See *Le Père Jacques, Martyr de la charité* (Etudes Carmélitaines, 1947).

Before the clothing of the condemned was removed, I saw Pastor Bonhoeffer on his knees before his God in intense prayer. The manner in which this extraordinarily likeable man prayed with total submission and certainty of being heard profoundly moved me. At the place of execution he prayed again, then he courageously climbed the gallows steps; death occurred within a few seconds. In fifty years of practice, I've never seen a man die so totally committed into the hands of God.[12]

The Germans also dearly cherish the memory of a fine figure of the spiritual resistance, Pastor Paul Schneider. Arrested in his parish for the courage of his sermons and his resistance to nazism, he was to perish mercilessly in a Buchenwald bunker on July 18, 1939. Often in the morning, when the prisoners were mustered on the assembly field, he pulled himself up to the high cell window and cried out to them, "Courage, comrades, Christ is living; fear not, only believe," or other biblical words, until his guards' blows silenced him. This attitude and this proclamation had a great impact on the camp, and he was called "the preacher of Buchenwald." I heard the report about him from an old German prisoner, a Communist, who came to participate in a special worship service at which I was presiding by invitation at Kloster Neuendorf (East Germany) in July 1975, and who, almost forty years later, still recalled with emotion the words of Pastor Schneider.

And how could we overlook, even if the example is outside the concentration camps themselves, the self-abnegation of Abbé Franz Stock, German chaplain of the Fresnes prison during the Occupation, carrying out his ministry and rendering innumerable services, at the risk of his life, to the interned patriots.[13]

But who could compile the list of these exceptional beings that

12. Eberhard Bethge, *Dietrich Bonhoeffer* (Geneva: Labor & Fides; also Paris: Le Centurion, 1969, p. 848.
13. René Closset, *L'aumônier de l'enfer, Franz Stock* (Salvator, 1964).

the infernal camp regime brought to light? These few references, to which others could be added, are intended only to attest to the existence of those who were an inspiration.

Personally, I still preserve in my mind the image of Albert Cappus. In this world of degradation and terror, in the midst of unnamed suffering, he gave his whole being; his soul had become transparent and radiant with light. I can only repeat what I wrote about him just after my liberation:

> Despite his weakness, his serenity was remarkable, and everybody, regardless of nationality, loved Albert. What he did and what he showed himself capable of doing in the hell of the concentration camp reflected pure charity. Yes, I have observed that there is a love stronger than hatred, and indeed I learned this secret, which had been revealed to Albert, my best friend.
> I knew, furthermore, that if God should grant him the grace to survive, he intended to consecrate his life to God's service. But, at the height of his suffering, his soul attained such purity that God judged him ready for another service.

Should I add that, as I observed how the Czech Georges Klouda—whom I knew to be Socialist and whom I believed to be agnostic—acted at Laura, the thought came to me that, if one were truly Christian, he ought to conduct himself with the same altruism? Thirty-one years later, upon rediscovering him, I was surprised to learn that he was a member of an evangelical congregation in Prague.

It is necessary also to call attention to the "Bible-searchers" or German Jehovah's Witnesses, interned as conscientious objectors. Wearing a purple triangle, they were grouped together in certain blocks at Buchenwald. Their deportment and their discipline were commensurate with their convictions and inspired great respect. W. Langhoff recounts how one of them brought death upon himself rather than say "Heil Hitler."[14] His martyrdom recalls the un-shakeable faith of the Christian legionnaires in Rome, who preferred to risk chains by responding "Christ is Lord" when they were expected to say "Caesar is Lord."

In general, the spiritual life of the believers was manifested by their recourse to prayer, as the following accounts confirm:

> Prayer was our daily weapon; it brightened the sad prison hours; it was our sustenance during the painful period of interrogation; it was our refuge at the moments when all else seemed to forsake us.[15]

> Despite all my anxiety, I tasted while praying of a strange serenity, a peace that let me believe that God, in the midst of all the suffering that would encumber me, would show me great favor and would grant me special grace.[16]

And from one of my deportation comrades:

> The general atmosphere was heavy; one sensed that the prisoners were weary, despairing of ever again seeing France. For December 8, 1943, we launched a Novena to ask the Holy Virgin to give us peace and not to let us die in the concentration camp. It was comforting to see how many youths, not usually practicing Catholics, would recite the rosary simply and respectfully while falling asleep in the evening, or they would recite it even during the workday. They gave the impression that they found a sort of consolation in it, grounds for hope and trust.[17]

14. *Les Soldats du marais* (Plon, 1937).

15. Pierre Suire, *Il fut un temps* (Niort, 1947), p. 28. Cf. also J. Hericourt, *Requiem à Buchenwald* (Paris: Apostolat des Editions, 1958).

16. Abbé Paul Parguel, *De mon presbytère aux bagnes nazis* (Spes Paris, 1946), p. 20.

17. Jean-Paul Garin, Dean of Medical Science at Lyons, *La Vie dure* (Audin Lyon, 1946), p. 95.

It was the simple, unadorned prayer of destitution that placed our burdens before God and asked for deliverance from them. Yvonne Pagniez records one of these prayers:

> Lord Jesus, we bring to you all our suffering, the anxiety of our souls, the profound misery of our bodies, for France. Save our dear country. . . . Lord, have mercy on those whom we love, and from whom we are separated, on those who suffer like us in the camps, on those who, weeping, wait for us at home. Let us all be reunited one day in joy. Nevertheless, may your will be done, and not ours.[18]

Certainly, it is instinctive to cry "help" when we're unhappy. But we truly learned again the prayer of intercession and the prayer of thanksgiving. We experienced the strength of the communion of the universal church. We felt ourselves uplifted by the prayer of those who were interceding for us. Michelet testifies:

> How can the collective prayers that surrounded me in block 26 be passed over in silence? If I had not felt literally sustained, uplifted by them, would I have persisted, as I did, in this determination not to let go?[19]

And Niemöller reports:

> I shall never forget what my father said during the last visit that he made me in the Gestapo office in the Oranienburg concentration camp. As he took leave of me, he said, "My child! the Eskimos of Canada and the Bataks of Sumatra send you their greetings, and they are praying for you."[20]

18. *Scènes de la vie* du bagne, p. 114.
19. *Rue de la Liberté*, p. 246.
20. Martin Niemöller, *De la culpabilité allemande* (Delachaux & Niestlé, 1946), p. 38.

The Christian life cannot be limited to personal piety; it needs communication and it draws its strength from communion. That is why some services, necessarily secret and always at risk, were organized by small groups. Such groups were begun in the prisons or at Compiègne, where it was still possible. And it is not without emotion that I recall the service that my eight cell mates had asked me to conduct on the first Sunday in the Toulouse prison. In the Compiègne camp, operated as a prisoner-of-war camp, where religious activities were tolerated and supervised under the protection of the Geneva Convention, Catholics, Protestants, and Orthodox knew an intense spiritual life that prepared them for the wilderness sojourn that was to follow.

In the concentration camps, only a few Bibles and missals, which were of great help, could be safeguarded. For lack of them, we tried to recall familiar biblical texts, Psalms, Sunday school songs. At Ravensbrück, "Catholics who could escape fatigue duty sometimes gathered to read the mass in a block on Sunday. Protestants gathered outside and commented on a verse."[21] Christians assembled in like manner in many other camps, very episodically of course, depending on circumstances, and always clandestinely. We did not let pass a single Christmas or Easter without feeling the need for commemorating the spiritual significance by assembling, though briefly, some Catholics and Protestants fraternally united, in some corner of the camp. Thus latrines could become sanctuaries while a comrade, sometimes Communist, kept watch for us.

The Catholics arranged to serve some Holy Communion wafers that priests had smuggled into the camp on their persons. They often performed astounding feats in order to give absolution to the dying, Communion to the faithful, and even to celebrate mass. I remember Abbé Amyot's joy at Osterhagen the day a comrade gave

21. Dr. Paulette Don Zimmet-Gazel, *Les conditions d'existence et l'état sanitaire dans les camps de concentration des femmes déportées en Allemagne* (Annemasse, 1949), p. 113.

him some raisins, received in a package, that he could bless to sig-
nify the lord's blood.

One evening in January 1945, a rite unprecedented in these parts
was observed at Osterhagen when, after having buried the body of
our friend Méchin outside the camp, the SS permitted me to pray
the Our Father over the open grave in the presence of our four comrades, gravediggers for the nonce.

In recalling the spiritual life in the concentration camps, one
must not clothe it in some sort of romanticism: it was as vacillating
as our physical life. We were poor men, beset with misery. Our men-
tal faculty was diminished by privation, our memory weakened, and
sometimes it was only with difficulty that I could recall the words of
the Our Father. To quote Henri Teitgen, respected president of the
Nancy Bar Association:

> All meditation, all oration, and all prayer become suffering, so
> difficult is it to wrest oneself from the bestiality which over-
> comes you from all sides and from the anguish which grips you
> without respite.[22]

But basically, if the means of expression were lacking, the faith was
there—a faith unadorned and simple, stripped of conventions and
artifice, a faith that the hours of anguish and doubt could make
vacillate but did not extinguish, and that reappeared in the darkest
moments. Faith is a mystery. I have proven almost concretely that
faith was given me; it did not come from myself.

Shall I dare confide that we knew certain privileged moments
when faith literally bore us up? That evening of August 26, 1944,
comes to mind: eight of us Frenchmen were condemned to die in a
violent manner. While we were locked in a barrack awaiting the
course of events, fear tightening the pit of the stomach, a Catholic
comrade and I received, at a given moment, the assurance that our

22. "Buchenwald 1944–1945," in *La Vie Intellectuelle* (Paris: July 1945).

lives were in God's hands. I prayed aloud for all of us. An unknown peace engulfed us. I hesitate to recount what constitutes a personal and incommunicable experience, and which may leave some skeptical. But I am convinced that experiencing the proximity of the Lord was a reality, not a phantasmagorical experience produced by terror. I vividly remember that at least two or three times in the course of this captivity, I received the grace of this exceptional relief, of this strength, and I shall even say of this joy in the bosom of the most profound distress. I have confirmed that others also confess to this kind of experience (Corrie Ten Boom, for example). Was this the coming of the Spirit, imparting that joy of which Christ spoke to his disciples as they approached Gethsemane, there to endure the most frightful agony?[23]

If we had a thirst for God, many of our comrades, as the opportunity arose in conversation, consciously or unconsciously demonstrated the desire to know Him better. Thus the concentration camps did not inhibit apostleship, all the more true because it was difficult. Abbé Parguel has explained:

> We sensed how eager all these men were to know and also to live that ideal incarnate in the Catholics, priests or laymen, and in the other Christians of the Resistance present in the camp.[24]

And Abbé G. Henocque has testified:

> I frequently had the good fortune of leading to God brave hearts who had preserved religious sentiments and, under the influence of the grave reflections that captivity suggested to them, were eager to become practicing Christians again. Other times, there were free thinkers, suddenly placed in the presence of great

23. John 15:11.
24. *De mon presbytère aux bagnes nazis*, p. 62.

problems of suffering and death, who were trying to find the light. How many came back to God in the milieu of this jail![25]

Abbé René Fraysse has cited the example of a young Breton who, after receiving instruction from a member of the Young Christian Workers, a Catholic organization, made his first Holy Communion in the camp.[26]

The thirst for God was sometimes given poetic expression, as in the following lines:

Travelers empty-handed, we entered here by order,
And, pilgrims of forced labor, we had to cross the border
To find You in this German camp, like us, poor and bare—
To find You, Lord, long lost to us since long-lost days more fair,
But here You are, enshrined in grief, our misery to share.[27]

Is it possible to discern the evolution of faith and of the Christian life brought about by the shock of the concentration camp universe? When I returned from the camps, people said to me, "You must have had some very unusual experiences in that 'obscure night,' as St. John of the Cross would say; as you reflect, surely these experiences will be seen in the light of a new day." One poorly conceives to what extent we were enfeebled, empty beings. Concentration camps hardly provide leisure for internalizing. Theirs is a world where harmful powers abide, a world where evil rumbles, the world of the shadows of death, the death that attacks not only the body but also the soul.[28]

25. *Dans les antres de la Bête* (Paris: Durassié).
26. *De Francfort à Dachau* (Annonay: 1946), p. 42, n. 26.
27. Dr. Henri Duclos, in *Le Ciel est par dessus le camp*. Adapted by the translators.
28. See in particular Dean Charles Hauter's conclusion in *De l'Université aux camps de concentration, témoignages strasbourgeois* (Paris: Les Belles Lettres, 1947).

Certainly, it was an ascetic life from which we parted not necessarily better but more mature. Through the hardship of suffering, of extreme distress, many opened up to others through an altruism that is not natural. By nature, the being who is dying of hunger or of fear worries only about himself. Usually, suffering hardens; sometimes it liberates. When a spiritual liberation occurs, is it not sign and effect of the essential mystery of Christianity, the redemptive suffering of Christ?

I have also been asked if I have ever known doubt. How should we have escaped its insidious gnawing without being blind and deaf to the reality that encompassed us? How should we have been exonerated from the test of Job, or of John the Baptist in prison, asking if Jesus were truly the messenger in whom he must place complete confidence? I see again a brother who said to me one day when we were nearing the breaking point, "Do you believe that He suffered as much as we are suffering?" Yes, one can cross these zones of shadow, and even of darkness, where, rejoining the Christ in agony until the end of the world, as Pascal said, one cries, "My God, why hast Thou forsaken me?" But communion in the mystery of the cross—at the same time scandal and compassion (in its etymological sense of suffering together)—sustains hope and faith. Among the books born of the hardship of the extermination camps, André Neher's account is certainly one of the richest in theological and spiritual profundity.[29] Few books have touched me as that one. The author described in it, with an extreme sensitivity, what the ordeal of God's silence is—that it is not necessarily an absence—and how hope against all hope surged from the absolute abandonment: from the defeat at Auschwitz sprang forth Hope.

It is important to note that Christians in the camps, as in the Resistance, were brought together with people (Communists in par-

29. *L'exil de la parole. Du silence biblique au silence d'Auschwitz* (Le Seuil, 1970).

ticular) of a different social and cultural background and therefore with a different frame of reference—people with whom until then they had rarely had occasion to associate. Thus Jacques Duquesne comments:

> At Dachau, Edmond Michelet becomes the friend of an old Communist militant, Germain Auboiroux. When Michelet becomes ill, Auboiroux takes it upon himself to substitute for him a half-hour each morning as a temporary replacement in the chapel. At Mauthausen some Communists gave Father Riquet suitable vestments, a rosary, and a missal; hence he will speak of "those Red friendships which I surely hope never to have to deny." At Neuengamme, Abbé Parguel finds Communists from the Voves camp interned by the Daladier Government at the beginning of the war and released to the Gestapo by the Vichy Government. "It is among these Communists," he will say afterwards, "that I could see some of the finest examples of fraternity set forth."[30]

There are many other references of the same nature.

This discovery bore within itself the apostolic evolution of the Church toward pluralism. Abbé Parguel observes:

> We have felt the necessity of a renewal of our apostleship. How could the Christian's life inspire this too widespread form of modern Christianity in which the priest, by his life style, his spirit, his reflexes, is a bourgeois even if he is poor—in which, immured in his presbytery and his church, imprisoned in a world of outdated customs, he no longer has any real contact with the human masses that await the message of the gospel.[31]

30. *Les catholiques français sous l'occupation* (1966), p. 385.
31. *De mon presbytère aux bagnes nazis*, p. 42.

Abbé René Fraysse predicts:

> Together we shall work out great dreams of apostleship, magnificent plans. The corrupt, inhuman social order known to the prewar era will be replaced by a more fraternal, more human, more Christian order. We comment on the last encyclicals, we speak of deproletarization, of revision of property rights. In liturgy, change is no less revolutionary.[32]

In the same way, the mutual acquaintance of Catholics and Protestants who find themselves in agreement on the essentials has certainly contributed to the development of ecumenical relations.

I have no knowledge of any calling to the priesthood that the deportation could have incited. If personally I felt confirmed in my pastoral calling and undertook theological studies upon my return, I can attest that among our group of young Protestants who united at Compiègne around Pastor Heuzé, three other comrades had heard this call to the ministry of the Gospel; of them only André Guyonnaud returned and could answer the call.

To conclude soberly, I should like to say that this camp experience revealed to us to what extent we, members of the human species, are interdependent. Is there a specific characteristic of Christian conduct? If so, perhaps it is, as Edmond Michelet notes, "this grace of the transfiguration of our suffering and that, staggering, of the disarming of hatred"; and I shall add: a certain element of hope—in any case not some sort of superiority that would isolate us from our brothers, other men. I am struck by the friendship that unites many survivors after so many years, by their desire not to forget, certainly, but also to proceed past this period. Believers and nonbelievers, they are not devoured by hate, by a thirst for vengeance, but in the measure of their means they want to work for peace, for greater justice, and for the promotion of human rights.

32. *De Francfort à Dachau.*

Aimé Bonifas, a retired pastor of the French Reformed Church, resides in Nîmes, France. He is a member of the Academy of Nîmes, president of the YMCA Men's Club, and a co-founder of the Nîmes chapter of Amnesty International as well as of the Nîmes chapter of ACAT. He is also a member of the National Federation of Deportees, Prisoners, Resisters, and Patriots. Pastor Bonifas lectures and writes on behalf of those of his generation whose voices were prematurely silenced and in the interest of the oppressed throughout the world. As an activist who opposes injustice and who seeks peace and security for all, he participates in conferences convened in Western Europe, Eastern Europe, and the United States to address the issues of human rights.

Mildred M. Van Sice, former teacher of English, is a free-lance translator from French to English, an associate member of the American Translators Association, a council member of the Alliance Française of Wilmington, Delaware, a braillist specializing in French transcriptions for the Delaware Division for the Visually Impaired, and a member of the National Braille Association.

Claude R. Foster, Jr., is professor of history at West Chester University in West Chester, Pennsylvania. He is a specialist in the history of the German Reformation. He has written many articles on Church-State relations and has co-edited collections of essays pertaining to the Holocaust. He frequently is invited to lecture at historical congresses in the United States and Europe, and each summer he conducts for Americans a Reformation seminar in the German Democratic Republic.